The True Story Of Kill Or Be Killed In The Real Old West

The Recollections And Personal Photos Of Frank "Pistol Pete" Eaton Old West Gunfighter and Lawman

Proudly Published By:

James A. Huebner

(Publisher's Note: Except for the above notification and my contact information, this memoir is preserved just the way it was typed almost a century ago on a ribbon typewriter)

Contact:

James A. Huebner
818 S.E. 4th. Street Suite 204
Ft. Lauderdale, Florida 33301
Phone: 941/376-1595
Email: jahuebner@comcast.net
www.OldWestLawmansForgottenMemoir.com

ACKNOWLEDGEMENT

My friend and partner, Eva Gillhouse, wrote this book. It was her idea and she did all the work. It's just the way I told it to her — it's all true — and I'll back her with both guns.

PISTOL PETE

DEDICATION

To the American Cowboy, who has played such a vital part in the progress of our great country and in the imagination of its people.

Contents

List of Photos

1 THE NEW HOME

FATHER

FATHER owned a livery, feed and sales stable, in Hartford, Connecticut, where I was born on October 26, 1860.

After the Civil War Father came home from the army, sold his business, and went out to Kansas — a new country in the Far West.

He went on the train, which was an adventure in itself in those days. Before he sent for Mother and us three children, he bought a farm and built a house.

He had a home ready for us, so we did not have many of the hardships of the earlier pioneers.

Father was about thirty-five years old at that time, six feet tall, and weighed about one hundred and eighty-five pounds.

He was a very strong man with rather short arms.

He had kind brown eyes, dark brown hair and a heavy brown mustache.

I was seven years old then, and I re-member just how my father looked; he always wore a blue flannel shirt, summer or winter, and a pair of blue jean pants with suspenders.

I loved my father.

He was always tolerant with other people and respected their opinions, but he had strong convictions and set ideas of right and wrong.

When he thought he was on the right side, he was a hard man to turn. Father was a soft-spoken man, never quarrelsome; it was hard to make him mad but once aroused he had a violent temper and you had better get away and let Nature supply the lightning rods!

1

Father met us at the train at Lawrence, Kansas. We were looking out the window, trying to see him; as the train slowed to a stop we caught sight of him.

He was standing by his team, holding their heads and rubbing their noses so they would not be afraid of the train. I started to rushfor the door, then went back and got my little sister by the hand. Mother had my baby brother in her arms and one of the other passengers helped her with some bundles and our valise.

Father hugged us and put my sister and me into the back of the wagon. Mother and my baby brother sat up on the seat with him.

I remember how he looked at her and said, "It's good to see you, Lizzie."

We stopped a couple of days about six miles out of Lawrence and visited some of Father's relatives.

Then, we drove on to our new home.

THE HOMESTEAD

Our home was in Osage County, Kansas, about thirty-eight miles southwest of Lawrence, at a place called Rock Springs, on the headwaters of the Red Woods Branch.

Four big springs of good water came together there and it was a famous watering place and campgrounds for grants and freighters. (A freighter was a teamster who hauled goods and supplies from the end of the railroad to out lying points.)

There had been an old hotel on the place but it was burned by William Clarke Quantrill and his men at the time they made the raid on Lawrence, Kansas.

Our house was built on the site of the ruins of the old hotel; it lay on a gentle slope of ground on the west bank of the stream about a hundred yards off the old Santa Fe Trail

THE SANTA FE TRAIL

The Santa Fe Trail was a great broad trail and the only real one in that part of the country at the time. It was a trade route, the first of the great transcontinental trails, between the East and West.

In 1821 a man named William Becknell freighted a load of goods by packhorses from Missouri to New Mexico.

The following year he made another trip from Franklin, Missouri, and arrived in Santa Fe, New Mexico, with twenty-one men and three wagonloads of goods, which he sold for a good profit. Becknell was known as "the father of the Santa Fe Trail."

Others soon followed — caravans began moving west starting from the Missouri River and it was called the Santa Fe Trail. Later, Independence, Missouri, became the official starting point.

Where we lived, in Kansas, the trail was lined with sunflowers; they were beautiful and they were also used for fuel. The stalks were so large they were chopped down and cut into stove lengths and burned for wood.

The flowers were dried and used for quick fires or for starting a fire.

The sunflowers provided the wagon trains and caravans with fuel when they stopped at the Rock Springs Camp Ground.

One of my earliest recollections is cutting down the sunflowers and watching the wagon trains on the trail.

WAGON TRAINS

Each wagon had its string of oxen hitched to it and the driver walked along on the left side of his team with his whip over his shoulder.

The driver was called a "bullwhacker." He was usually a young man and he drove from two to eight yoke of oxen. He wore a wide-brimmed hat and high-topped boots with broad heels. He walked by the side of his team most of the time and commanded them with a long bullwhip.

The whip was a braided lash, from twelve to fourteen feet long, with a broad buckskin popper on the end. The whip was about one and one-half inches thick where the whipstock was tied on and ran to a true taper to the size of your little finger, where the popper was fastened.

The whipstock, or handle, was of shaved hickory and was four or five feet long. From the size of a pitchfork handle at the butt, the whipstock tapered like a billiard cue, to the size of a man's finger where the whip was fastened on.

A good bullwhacker could kill a wolf or rattlesnake with his whip and the crack of his whip was louder than a shot from a forty-five.

There was a trail boss, too, or an "emigrant boss" as he was sometimes called. He was a man who had to know his job.

He was always an old plainsman. The more he knew of outlaws, Indians and the country he was traveling, the better he was.

4

His word was law; he was in absolute control of the whole outfit.

The emigrant boss knew the destination of his wagon train and his job was to get them through.

When they arrived his job was done.

There never was a prettier sight than ten or twenty big wagons with boxes as high as your chin all covered over with white wagon sheets.

Women and children looked out both ends of the wagon; the boys and some of the men drove the cattle and horses along in the rear.

Mounted and armed men rode on the front and flanks, looking for any sign of danger.

The whole outfit, moving slowly along the trail, once seen could never be forgotten.

NEIGHBORS

There was a faint trail that branched off the Santa Fe Trail just east of our house; it ran northeast to Ottawa, Kansas.

All the rest was open prairie country covered with tall grass. When we wanted to go anywhere we forked our horse and made our own trail.

All the settlements were on the streams where water was plentiful. North of us about five miles there were a dozen farms on the creek. There was a post office five miles northeast of us, at a small settlement called Twin Mounds.

There were several small towns on the prairie; the nearest was Hundred-Ten — so named because it was one hundred and ten miles from the Missouri line.

Then there were Carbondale, Lyndon, Ridgeway and Ottawa.

George Saffles was our nearest neighbor — he lived about half a mile south; Marcus Whittenburg lived a little farther on. Mose Beaman, Arthur Duffy and his brother Pete lived about six or eight miles south. Bill Montcastle and Si Dodder were east of our place four miles.

Across the Rock Springs draw, about a half mile away, was the Campsey place. The Campseys were bad and their friends were bad. They had belonged to the Quantrill Raiders during the Civil War and their place was a hangout for men of shady reputation.

There were two brothers, Doc and John Ferber, who spent most of their time at the Campsey place, but the place belonged to Shannon Campsey and his three brothers, Jim, Jonce and Wyley.

SIGNALS

We were right on the edge of the open range.

Nearby were some limestone bluffs, full of rattlesnakes. We could climb on top of a bluff and see as far as the eye could reach.

By putting up a red flag we could have a band of fifteen or twenty armed men in a very short time and more coming as fast as their horses could carry them.

Father was always on the lookout for all signals.

He would come into the house, put on his gun belt, take down his rifle, and in his quiet way he would say to Mother, "There is a meeting, Lizzie."

Then he would kiss her and us children and ride away to the gathering place and Mother would go into the bedroom and kneel by the bed and pray.

TWO FACTIONS

It was directly after the close of the Civil War and the country was sparsely settled at that time.

Veterans of the Union and Confederate Armies were about equal in number among the settlers.

There was still a lot of bitterness among them over the war and it was only natural that there were two different factions striving for control.

In Kansas after the Civil War, the Vigilantes, like the Vigilance Committees in the entire Western states and territories, were organized to protect the citizens from a lawless element.

The Vigilantes were made up of Union men and a few hired gunmen, and were under the command of a Northern man named Mose Beaman.

Beaman, during the war, had been one of the Jennings Red Legs, a regiment of Jayhawkers in the Union Army, who saw service along the Kansas and Missouri line.

On the other side were the Regulators, armed men organized in some of the Southern states and along the Border States, to obstruct the activities of the freedmen's organizations.

They usually rode at night, sometimes in disguise. They were a sort of forerunner of the Ku Klux Klan, but they were not well organized and lacked a definite aim.

The Regulators were composed of Southern men and some hired gunmen, and were led by Si Dodder.

They had been able to get some of their men elected to office and were having things pretty much their own way— so it was a bad situation

Si Dodder had a habit of stealing some of the horses and cattle from the emigrant trains that were camped in his neighborhood.

He would hide them; then collect a reward for finding them. When he drove them back to the owners and they paid the reward, he would turn some of their other stock loose, later demanding damages because they ran over his hay land.

There was a lot of travel and he was doing fairly well until the Vigilantes got on to it and started watching him.

THE BULLWHACKER

One day a young man driving three yoke of oxen camped at the spring by the side of the road.

He had made a fire of dead sunflowers and dried cow chips and was cooking his dinner when Si Dodder came by and tried to scare his cattle but they were chained to the wheels of the big wagon and could not break away.

The bullwhacker grabbed his whip and nearly whipped Si Dodder to death.

Just then some of Si's men came along and took him home and swore out a warrant for the bullwhacker.

They took him up before old man Wadsworth, who was Justice of the Peace and also one of Si's strongest henchmen, with instructions to fine him his wagon and three yoke of oxen.

VIOLENCE

Mother had gone to Mrs. Saffles's as midwife and Father was down in the orchard hoeing weeds out of the gooseberries.

I was trying to catch a gopher and had him in a hole, when Mose Beaman and about a dozen other mounted men came riding up in a hurry.

"Get your horse and guns, Frank," he called to my father. "The Vigilantes are riding!"

Father looked at me. "What shall I do with the boy? Can't leave him here alone."

"Never mind," says Mose, "hand him up here and we will begin his education right now!"

Father swung me up to Mose who put me down behind him and told me to hang on.

Father had his horse ready and in a few minutes he came out of the house with his rifle, buckling on his gun. I got both hands in Mose's gun belt and hung on for dear life.

I had ridden the workhorses down to the spring for water. I had been thrown from every calf, colt and hog on the place. But this was different!

This was excitement, adventure, maybe violence! I had never seen any violence. I thought about the many times I had watched the men ride away, their faces grim and set.

Now I was going with them!

With all my seven years of experience, I was one of them!

As we rode along Mose told of Si Dodder's fight with the bull whacker. "Are we going to hang Dodder?" someone asked.

9

"Not yet," said Mose. "Our job, now, is to turn the bullwhacker loose. A couple of our men are taking his outfit wagon and oxen — over to Hundred-Ten Creek. They will wait there for him until we send him in, which won't be long now."

About that time, Arthur Duffy and a group of twenty-five or thirty men, who had met at his house in answer to his signals, came in across the prairie and joined us.

Judge Wadsworth was holding court in a small rock house by a big spring. There was a bunch of horses tied to the willow trees around the spring but no men were in sight.

"They must all be in the house," said Mose, "and that is all the better for us."

All the men knew just what to do. They surrounded the house and placed guards at all the doors and windows.

Then Mose and the rest of the men went into the house. I was put in the corner and told to lie down on the floor if there was any shooting.

Mose walked deliberately across the room and lit his pipe with a coal of fire from the hearth.

He was a large man with a heavy body, and he didn't know the meaning of fear. He was square and honest and believed in settling his difficulties immediately, without quarreling.

Judge Wadsworth was a big man too, but overbearing and dishonest, put into office by a lawless element for his own protection.

His eyes were black and set close together; he had lots of thick black hair, a long beak nose and a thick, heavy neck. He was watching Mose, with his shoulders hunched, as though he were ready to spring.

Mose took a long draw on his pipe; it was a clay pipe with a long cane stem. He looked the judge square in the eye and threw his hat into one corner of the room and his coat into the other.

Then, still looking him in the eye, he walked over in front of him and banged his fist on the table saying, "This court is now adjourned!"

"Who are you," cried Wadsworth, "that you are usurping the proceedings of a court of justice?"

Reaching over and giving the judge's nose a vigorous twist Mose replied, "I am Mose Beaman, by God!"

The judge looked around. The room was full of armed men and the door and windows were bristling with rifle barrels.

The Regulators were stacking their guns in one corner. Judge Wadsworth unbuckled his belt and threw his guns with the others.

Taking the bullwhacker by the arm Mose led him out where Marcus Whittenburg was holding a bunch of horses.

Mose brought out his own sorrel, bald-faced mare and giving the reins to the bullwhacker said, "Now, mister, you get on that plug and ride to Hundred-Ten, where you will find your outfit waiting for you. Give the boys this horse and take your oxen and wagon and get the hell out of here! And if you ever come back bring your guns and a few friends in case we haven't got cleaned up around here."

The grateful bullwhacker thanked him and rode off in the direction of Hundred-Ten.

After looking around for Si Dodder and not finding him Mose Beaman started giving the judge some good advice, but Wadsworth was in a fighting mood.

It didn't last long for Beaman just kicked and booted that judge all over hell!

Then the Vigilantes got on their horses and rode away, leaving the judge swearing at the top of his voice while trying to stop his nose from bleeding.

THE FIGHT

A few days later Eli Emery came by our house and told father that the two men had met on the prairie and fought it out. Wadsworth was at home, and Doc Ferber was trying to keep him alive.

When the two men met they hung their guns on their saddle horns, took off their coats, and fought barehanded.

Wadsworth knew Mose Beaman could outshoot him but he thought he could whip him with his fists.

He was wrong!

They must have fought like hell, for Beaman had beaten him senseless. The grass was high and Beaman had then tied Wadsworth's pony to his master's foot to keep the wolves away and so his friends could find him, or so his pony wouldn't stray and he would have a way to get home when he regained his senses.

Mose had got on his horse and started home, but his eyes swelled shut and the horse, used to stopping at Duffy's, turned in and stopped at the hitch rack.

Mose thought he was home and got off his horse and went to hunting for the yard gate.

Arthur Duffy was sitting on the porch, and he saw there was something wrong with Mose; he got up and went out to where he was groping along the fence and when he saw Mose's face, he exclaimed, "Good God, Mose, what have you been up to?"

"Well," said Mose, "you know old Wad and I had an argument at the trial the other day and we finished it a while ago. I left old Wad out there in the grass and started home while I could still see but my damned eyes swelled shut and the pony stopped here and here I am."

Arthur Duffy took him home and then went after Wadsworth. He found him covered with green flies and took him home and told Doc Ferber.

Doc worked on him all night, cleaning off the flyblow, but it was no use; Wadsworth died the next day and they buried him in the Willow Spring graveyard.

There was a big crowd of Vigilantes at the funeral and among them were Pete and Arthur Duffy.

As we walked away from the grave I heard Arthur say, "May the devil fly away with him and dogs defile his grave! But he had good nerve and he was a good fighting man."

2 TRAGEDY

WOOD was scarce, so father and Perry Manning took their teams and went over to Carbondale after a load of coal.

When they got there they found the sheriff from Ottawa and a couple of men from Burlingame looking for some stolen horses.

After they had described the horses Perry

Manning said, "I saw those horses as we came over this morning."

"Where were they?" asked the sheriff.

"In Shannon Campsey's corral!" replied Manning.

"Where is the place?"

"Out at Rock Springs Camp on the east side of the ravine."

"How far?"

"About ten miles."

"All right, boys, let's get going," said the sheriff and he and the two other men rode on.

Shannon Campsey lived on the east side of the Rock Springs draw. The camp ground and the spring, on the west side of the draw, were on my father's land and all the neighbors used the spring and the branch for water for the stock and also for their homes.

Beginning of Trouble

I had my little ax and was out beside the trail chopping down the sunflowers and cutting them into stove lengths, when the sheriff and his posse rode up and stopped to question me.

"Hello, son," said the sheriff, "is this where Shan Campsey lives?"

"No sir," I said. "He lives in that house across the creek."

"Who lives here?"

"We do," I said.

"What is your father's name?" asked the sheriff.

"His name is Frank Eaton."

"And what is your name?"

"My name is Frank Eaton and my sister's name is Lizzie and the baby is Jean." I was just getting acquainted.

"How many men are there over at that Campsey place?" he asked.

"There are four, Jim and Jonce, Shannon and Wyley Campsey; and I saw Doc and John Ferber ride up there a little while ago."

The posse rode on and Mother and I stood out in the yard and watched them.

Shannon Campsey was riding the horses down to water when they met him. They arrested him right on one of the stolen horses and he gave up without any trouble.

Then he asked to go to the house to get his hat and the sheriff told him to go ahead.

The sheriff and his posse were getting the horses tied and ready to lead when Shan came out of the house with five other men and covered them.

16

Shan ordered them to throw down their guns and dismount. The six of them started the sheriff and his posse down the back trail, at gunpoint, while they took their saddle horses, along with the stolen horses, and rode off in the direction of Si Dodder's place.

The sheriff came back to our house and asked where they could get help. Mother told him to go to Arthur Duffy's or Mose Beaman's, or else to Marcus Whittenburg's.

It was only three miles to Whittenburg's, so they went there.

When Father and Perry Manning came home Mother told them what had happened and they knew there was going to be trouble. Manning started home at once.

There was no one at the Campsey place when he passed there, but about half a mile beyond someone shot his hat off.

He got out his gun and had a hot time until his team started to run and took him out of danger.

Father unloaded the coal and turned his team in the lot.

After supper he thought the Vigilantes might ride so he tied up his saddle horse to have him ready.

Then we sat and talked until bedtime.

HORSEMEN

Mother had gone to bed and Father and I had taken off our boots when we heard the sound of running horses and Father said, "There comes Mose and the boys now; they are early, aren't they?"

I ran to the door just as the horses stopped.

A man called for Father, who was right behind me.

17

There was a burst of gunfire and my father fell to the floor with six bullets through him.

I fell on his body screaming. One of the men got off his horse and pulled me away. He kicked me and hit me with his riding whip.

Then he emptied his gun into my father's body and cried, "Take that, you God-damn Yankee!"

Then they galloped away; but I had seen their faces. They were the four Campseys and the two Ferbers.

THE VIGILANTES

Our nearest neighbor was George Saffles, who lived about a half mile away, and Mother sent me to get him.

Just as we got back another body of horsemen rode up and Mose Beaman came in the door. I ran to him crying, "Oh, Mr. Beaman, they killed my father!"

He put his hand on my shoulder and spoke kindly. "Who killed him, son?"

"The Campseys and the Ferbers!"

Mose waited no longer but sent Arthur Duffy and all the others on the trail while he stayed to help us.

He went to Hundred-Ten and came back with a coffin and some more men. He did everything he could.

They buried my father in a cemetery at Twin Mounds. The coffin was lowered and the last clod of dirt was thrown on top.

As we turned to leave, a column of black smoke arose in the direction of Si Dodder's place, and I saw Mose look at Perry Manning and nod his head.

But nothing could bring back my father!

Mose went home with us and helped with the chores and told Mother not to worry: he would come every day and help her with the work.

When he was ready to leave he took my right hand in his, placed his left hand on my head and, looking straight into my eyes, said solemnly: "My boy, may an old man's curse rest upon you, if you do not try to avenge your father!"

"I will, Mr. Beaman! Just as soon as I am big enough and learn more about guns and shooting."

"Don't worry about guns and shooting," said Mose, "I will tend to that part. I want you to be good for the job ahead of you or you may not get it all done. You must never stop until they are all accounted for!"

GUNS

The next day Mose brought me a navy revolver.

The army and navy revolvers were the most popular guns in those days. "I brought the navy gun, son," Mose said, "because it is lighter than the army and the barrel is a little shorter. I think it will be better for you." It was about eight inches long, and the army gun had about a nine-inch barrel.

The army and navy guns were six-shooters. Mose fired the gun, and then held it for me to see.

"Now after the shot is fired and the gun is cocked, the chamber revolves and brings a new load under the hammer. That is why they are called revolvers."

There was an old gun, before the revolver, called the pepperbox gun, in, which the whole barrel revolved. But it went out when the revolver came in.

If these guns seem crude, remember that at that time there was no better weapon; it was a matter of knowing how to use them effectively.

You know the old flint arrow gave the Indian supremacy over man and beast.

It wasn't much of a weapon compared to the atom bomb, but at that time the bow and arrow was the best weapon available and the Indian knew how to use it

MOLDING BULLETS

All the guns used to be cap-and-ball guns — there were no cartridge guns in those days — and we made our own ammunition.

A couple of days after Mose brought me the gun he rode in and when he got off his horse he took some things out of his saddlebags, saying, "Today I am going to start teaching you to mold bullets."

I was very happy about that and looked to see what he had brought.

There was a can of gunpowder, three boxes of caps, a lot of lead, a pair of bullet molds and a melting ladle.

We put the stuff on a bench beside the house and built a small fire.

Mose put some lead into the ladle, then put it on the fire to melt; when it was hot he poured it into the bullet mold and let it set just a few seconds, then he dropped out the molded bullet.

I watched him: as soon as he had finished one he closed the mold and poured it full of lead again.

They were perfect but they sure were hot. We had to wait until they were cool enough to handle, then we cut the neck off and the bullet was ready to use. Mose said, "Always save the neck and use it again, for lead is scarce."

Then he let me fill the mold while he watched.

LOADING A CAP-AND-BALL GUN

Mose told me that as soon as I could mold the bullets by myself he would teach me how to load and fire my gun and sight a target. You had to get the knack of loading a cap-and-ball gun to be fast about it.

We used to keep the gunpowder in a powder horn, to keep it dry. We wore it fastened to a strap that hung over our shoulder. On the small end of the horn was a removable cover, called the charger — the charger was a measure.

In a few days I had a nice stack of perfect bullets for Mose to look at when he came. He inspected them carefully, then patted me on the shoulder and said, "That's fine, son. Now get your powder horn and I will show you how to load your gun."

I brought my powder horn and my gun and Mose loaded his gun as he showed me how.

"First," he said, "You pour the gunpowder out of the powder horn into the charger. When the charger is full that's how much powder it takes to fire the bullet. Then you pour the powder into the chamber of the revolver; now put in the molded bullet and ram it down with your ramrod; then put the cap on and you are ready to go."

I had done everything just as Mose had, while he was talking, and I was proud when he looked at my gun and said, "That's fine, son."

LEARNING TO SHOOT

Hardly a day passed but Mose was there to go on with my lessons. Patiently he taught me the first steps.

Then one day he saw me sight a small jug, on a fence post thirty feet away, empty my gun and hit it with the last shot.

21

He taught me always to be careful in loading and handling my gun. I will never forget his words, "Never aim your gun at anything but what you want to kill!"

He told me always to shoot at least ten or twenty shots a day. He gave me a belt and holster and fitted them to me.

He taught me how to draw and shoot without sighting along the barrel of the gun. "You must get used to pointing your gun like you would your finger," he said. "Look at your target instead of the sights. It may take a long time to master your gun but keep at it and you can shoot with the best of them for you have it in you. Learn to use your left hand part of the time. When you get good with it, I will give you another gun."

"Another thing," Mose said earnestly, "when you are older never take a drink of whisky and never gamble, for that would hurt your eyesight and your nerves. You will need them both for the job ahead of you."

I was only eight years old but I gave Mose my word. Gravely, he shook my hand, mounted his horse and rode away.

My days were spent helping Mother and learning to shoot with both hands.

Mose kept me supplied with ammunition and in the evenings I molded bullets and put them into the bullet pouch he had given me.

TWO GUNS

There were hundreds of rattlesnakes along the limestone ledges of the surrounding region. I had a box full of rattles cut from the snakes I had shot.

One day when Mose came to watch me I showed him how I could shoot a snake's head off with either hand.

True to his promise he brought me another gun, belt and holster complete. It was the same size as the first one and the same molds would make bullets for both guns.

I was proud of my two guns and felt I had lived up to what Mose expected of me. Times were very hard for the snakes after that, but we never killed game unless we needed it for food.

All the guns on the place were cleaned and loaded every day.

But the Campseys and the Ferbers had gone and so had Si Dodder.

3 GROWING UP

"TEXAS FEVER"

THE next year was the year 1869. In the spring, after the grass was good, the Texas herds of cattle came along the Santa Fe Trail.

One herd had with them a young buffalo it was the first buffalo I had ever seen and it was fairly tame, so I got a good look at it. How I wanted to own that buffalo!

After the third herd had gone by, the native cattle began dying of the "Texas fever" all along the Santa Fe Trail.

When the next herd came up from Texas they were met by a crowd of armed men and the owners were forced to turn and drive the cattle back. But the damage had been done.

By fall nearly everyone along the trail had lost his entire herd.

Our cattle were all dead. The herds belonging to Mose Beaman, Arthur Duffy, Perry Manning, Marcus Whittenburg and George Saffles were completely wiped out. There was nothing left but sad memories and dry cowhides.

MOTHER

That same fall Mother married a man by the name of J. N. Goodhue. He was a good man and I liked him.

Mother was a wonderful woman and she was beautiful, too. She had brown hair that was long and wavy, big dancing brown eyes and a happy disposition.

She was slender, of medium height, very active and ambitious.

An excellent cook and homemaker, she fairly worshiped her family. She was a devout Christian and a member of the Episcopal Church.

Shortly after my mother married Mr. Goodhue they sold the farm and moved to southern Kansas. We settled on Onion Creek, west of Coffeyville, Kansas.

COFFEYVILLE

Coffeyville was a thriving little town and a shipping point for the cattle from the Indian Territory.

It was a wide-open Old West border town, in those days, full of saloons and gambling halls.

Nick Martin had one of the saloons, on the Grand Plaza.

Dutch Plover owned the Southern Hotel and a livery stable south of the hotel.

Ford and Lang had a furniture store.

Reed Brothers, Wells Brothers, Kimball and Kellogg were some of the grocery stores.

T. B. Eldridge ran the bank, and a hotel called the Eldridge House.

A man named Peffer published the newspaper, the Coffeyville Journal.

Mr. Peffer was a distinguished looking old gentleman with a long white beard. Later he was elected a member of the Kansas Legislature on the Populist ticket.

There were three doctors, named Graham, Frazier and Tanner, and all of them had a good practice.

There were a score or more of small firms all doing a thriving business.

A man by the name of Mobley had a big water mill down by the water tank in the south part of town on the Verdigris River.

The railroad stopped about three miles south of town at the state line; that was where the stockyards were located.

There was a small town there called Parker,

but all the business was done at Coffeyville.

THE BENDERS

It was near Coffeyville that the notorious Bender family were captured by armed men and, according to legend, driven into the quicksand of the Arkansas River.

I remember the Benders, but all I ever knew about what happened to them I learned by snooping and by accident.

The Benders — old man Bender, his son John, and a daughter, Kate Bender ran a lodging house on the main traveled road north of Coffeyville. Lots of people stopped there and many were never seen or heard from again.

One morning I was down at the barn currying the horses.

Mother was sick, and my stepfather was up at the house. Ben Saffles, who stayed with us, was down at the creek, looking after the fish lines, when Bill and Oscar Luce came riding up and asked for Ben, who about the same time came up from the creek. He had a couple of catfish; he told me to take them up to the house and bring down his gun.

When I came back with the gun he had his horse saddled up and he rode off with Bill and Oscar, who were also Vigilantes.

He was gone three days before he came back.

He came in the afternoon, and I had curried the horses, cleaned out the barn and was out behind the barn resting.

KATE BENDER'S GUN

My stepfather was down at the barn and he thought I had gone to the creek to set some lines. I heard him say to Ben, "How did you make it?"

Ben answered, "All right." I was curious about where Ben and the other two men had gone, anyway, so I looked through a crack in the barn.

My stepfather said, "Did you have any trouble with them?"

"John and the old man were gentle as milk cows, but Kate fought like the devil.

Look here!" Ben raised his left arm and there was a bandage where a bullet had gone through the flesh. He was all bloody and bandaged up.

"That was a close call," said my stepfather.

"Yes, and I've got the gun that made it," said Ben; "but don't let any of the boys know I have it or they will make me throw it away. It's the first gun that ever made a mark on me and I'm going to keep it."

He showed my stepfather a Colt revolver; all brass-mounted and engraved, a beautiful piece of work.

The gun, originally a cap-and-ball gun, had been changed into a cartridge gun. It shot about a thirty-eight shell —rather a long one, too. You could put in a long thirty-eight and still have room to spare.

I was looking through that crack in the barn all this time and if either of them had known it they would have kicked me all over the creek bank.

Ben put the gun into his pocket and said, "We didn't let anybody take anything away. Just put the whole thing in, horses, wagon and all."

Later, when we moved to Indian Territory, Ben gave me that gun and told me it had belonged to Kate Bender.

I had it for a long time; then a few years ago I gave it to Mary Chancy up at Salt Fork, Oklahoma, and she still has it.

THE BENDER SYSTEM

The detectives got some of the Vigilantes to help and they dug up the Bender yard and went over the house.

They found out how the Benders had handled their victims without any disturbance.

When they set them down to the table to eat they were sitting with their backs to a curtain, and their chairs right over a trap door. One of the men would knock the victim on the head through the curtain and drop him down the trap door into the cellar.

Then, it was said, Kate would go to the cellar and cut his throat and go over his body. Kate loved to see the blood run.

Kate was a pretty woman, too. I remember her.

I saw her in Parsons, Kansas, one time when

I was just a little boy.

She had sort of straw-color hair and it was thick and heavy. She was a large woman but she had a good figure.

Her eyes were blue but they had an ugly glitter in them some way that scared me; I never forgot them.

In the yard the detectives found a number of bodies and things that had belonged to the victims, like guns and canes.

Folks thought the Benders had money buried in the yard, but none was ever found. I think they had their money with them, but it didn't do them any good.

None of the Vigilantes ever talked about it and no one can say what happened to the Benders for the ones who were there never told. So I don't know about that story, that the Vigilantes forced them into the quicksand. Of course, the Arkansas River has a lot of quicksand.

All the Vigilantes are dead now. One of them used to live here in Perkins. His name was Bird Porter, he helped capture the Benders and could have told a lot if he had wanted to but he never did.

About all the Vigilantes I remember were: my step-father, J. N. Goodhue; Ben Saffles; Mr. Peffer, the editor of the newspaper in Coffeyville; Colonel Osborne; Bob Chestnut; and Abe and Tom Mobley, whose father had the water mill down on the Verdigris River.

WE MOVE AGAIN

We lived there on Onion Creek for a while and then moved out on Cheyenne Creek, east and north of the town of Caney, Kansas.

At that time Caney consisted of a store owned by Jim White and his brother, a blacksmith shop belonging to old man Howard, and six or eight houses.

My sister, Lizzie, married Ben Saffles there and they settled on the Lee Boak place, adjoining ours.

By this time we had a little half-sister, Flora, whom my brother Jean and I fairly worshiped. She was a pretty little blue-eyed, yellow-haired girl and she loved to go for long walks with us down on the creek in the timber.

She always came home with her little apron full of flowers and acorns and all kinds of things we found for her.

We taught her the different kinds of trees and she always took home a leaf from each one of them to learn the difference in their form and color. She loved all the pretty varieties of grass and weeds.

She never forgot any of them, but she liked the stinging nettles best of all.

THE CHEROKEE NATION

We lived there near Cancy, Kansas, about three years and then moved down into the Indian Territory.

In those days that part of the territory was called the Nation — the Cherokee Nation.

We located about three miles south of where Bartlesville, Oklahoma, now stands. There was no town there at that time.

Mr. Goodhue, my stepfather, took up a lease from an Indian named Jesse Thompson.

In those days the Indian Territory all belonged to the Indians and anyone else who wanted to work or farm in the Territory had to have a permit from the Indian Agency signed by an Indian who was held responsible for their conduct.

The Indian got the permit and it cost him fifty cents; the same kind of permit was used to hire help or to lease land.

The way the land was leased, a man would "break out" or clear say about fifty acres, and improve it — the improvement to pay for a five-year lease on the land.

At the end of the five years, he could take fifty acres more and improve it for the next five- year lease; or sometimes they just rented the land at the end of the five years.

Our land was on the south side of Sand Creek in the bend of a big U-shaped hill. One end of the hill was on Sand Creek, and the east end was on the Caney River.

The country abounded in game of all kinds — deer, turkey, prairie chickens, quail, panthers, bobcats, coon, 'possum and all kinds of squirrels and rabbits.

I was in my glory but had to be saving of my ammunition, for the nearest place we could get more was at Caney, twenty miles north, or Coffeyville, thirty-six miles northeast.

We went to town twice a year.

In the spring we took our winter catch of furs and pelts.

In the fall we went to buy provisions. We always got a sack of sugar and a sack of green coffee. There was no roasted coffee on the market in those days.

A few years later Arbuckle and Lion coffee came out in one pound paper bags, roasted and ready to grind, retailing for ten cents a pound.

There were always about thirty skeins of yarn for the women to knit stockings, a bolt of blue-jean cloth to make pants and jackets for the men, and a bolt of linsey cloth, a coarse cloth made of wool and cotton, for clothes for the women, a pair of shoes for the women and boots for the men, a can of gunpowder, ten boxes of caps and some lead to make bullets.

WOLF DOGS

My brother Jean and I hoed tobacco and corn, helped get up the wood and water. The Indians gave us three good hunting dogs that were half wolf. The Indians bred the female dogs to the wolves, and the pups were smart and made good fighters.

We had one dog that would set a deer just like a setter dog sets a quail.

Deer were not so wild then, for they were only killed for food. Sometimes they would lie still until we got within fifty yards of them before they would jump and run.

Our stepfather gave Jean and me each a light rifle and let us hunt together.

We were good woodsmen and could take care of ourselves almost anywhere. We killed squirrels and rabbits for meat and once in a while a deer or turkey.

And all the while I was getting to be a better shot.

MOTHER'S ADOPTED CALF

In the Cherokee Nation all the stock ran out on the open range; we had to have a fence around the house to keep the hogs and cattle out of the kitchen and off the front porch, or gallery, as it was commonly called.

The barn and corncribs were fenced in, as well as all other places where we did not want the stock to run.

We had our house, smokehouse, all the outbuildings and the ash hopper inside a high rail fence.

The ash hopper was a container for wood ashes. It was made so that when we poured water over them the lye from the ashes ran out through

33

a trough. The lye was used in soap that was made from the cracklings after the lard was rendered out.

The fence enclosed the garden, the well and the flower garden, and there were steps to go over at the front and back.

My mother and sister Flora had lots of beautiful flowers.

There were zinnias, asters, bachelor buttons and many other kinds. The fence was covered with morning glories, ivy and bittersweet berries.

That garden was the thorn in the side of Jean and me for it was our job to grub out the weeds and grass and keep the soil loose and mellow.

It was lots more fun to take our rifles and go hunting than to take the hoe and work in the flowers and vegetables.

But it had to be done, so we kept it in fine shape, for we knew there would be no hunting while there were any weeds in the garden.

One spring an old cow died and left a little calf.

Mother adopted the little thing, took it in the yard and fed it milk and table scraps. It lived, and outgrew every other calf in the country.

Jean and I fenced the flowers off from the yard so the calf would not trample them, kept fresh water in the trough for it to drink — and in the fall it was bigger than a common yearling.

We had every Sunday to do as we pleased. There were no churches or Sunday schools. Sometimes we would go hunting and sometimes ride wild ponies or cattle.

We rode everything on the place.

One Sunday we had finished fixing the fence and were cleaning our guns.

Mother was out in the shed kitchen washing the milk pans, which she kept in the shed on a long bench where the sun would shine on them.

As she worked she sang that old hymn — In the sweet by-and-by . . .

When Jean and I finished cleaning our guns we hung them in their places.

We were at the well washing our hands when Mother's pet calf came up and began begging for some water.

We gave it to her and an idea struck us both at the same time. We looked at each other and Jean said to me, "If you will keep her from riding around where Mother is I will ride her to a finish." We had never been on her back. She was really Mother's pet!

We rubbed her neck till she shut her eyes. I whispered, "All right, hop on!" Jean piled on and got settled before the calf knew what had

happened. Then she jerked loose from me and went to bucking like a real bronco.

Jean stayed right with her.

After a turn around the flower garden she heard Mother singing and headed for the shed.

Mother was scouring the milk strainer when Jean and the calf came in, ran over the milk pans and upset the bench.

I was hanging on to the calf's tail trying to turn her from the shed, for I knew there was going to be trouble if Mother caught us riding that calf!

But I couldn't turn her, and neither could Jean. We all ran over the bench full of pans and buckets.

Mother threw up both hands, with the strainer in one and the scouring rag in the other. She gave a scream you could hear for a mile.

The calf ran right up to her and Jean slid off.

He and I ran around the corner of the shed as fast as we could go and the calf ran around Mother and stopped her bucking and went to drinking the dishwater and begging for biscuits.

We were looking through a crack to see how things were going when Mother called us.

We came out as sober as judges, and she looked at us a long time without speaking; then she said, "Young gentlemen, I want you to understand this calf is no saddle pony, and the next time you bother her I will get me a good hickory and you will sleep on your faces and take your meals standing up for a week when I am through with you.

Now gather up those pans and buckets, put the bench up, wash and scour all that tin ware and put it where it belongs. Clean everything up well, then you can go down to the creek, take a bath and change your clothes and behave yourselves the rest of the day."

She sat down on the end of a log on the woodpile and watched us; and that damned calf stood right there beside her.

RIDING THE CATTLE ON SUNDAY

On another Sunday morning, not long after, Jean and I had milked the cows, strained the milk and put it away.

Mother told us we could not go hunting for there was plenty of meat to last all week and we never killed the game unless we needed the meat.

Mother said we had better stay home and rest up while we could for there was a hard week ahead of us husking corn.

It was not what we had planned but we had to take it so we put our guns away, changed our clothes and went down to the straw stack. We

36

climbed up on top of it and were just lying there when Jess Hymer, one of the neighbor boys, rode up.

He climbed up on the straw stack and we all lay there watching the cattle. When an old steer got his head in a hole in the fence so he could not see us we would jump on his back and ride him.

Nearby in the calf pen was a large haystack with a rail fence around it. At one place the corner of the fence came close to the haystack with room for only one calf to go by at a time.

After riding the steers for a while we all went over to the calf lot.

Each got on a calf to see who could stay the longest.

The calves were running and bucking and finally started around the stack.

Jess Hymer's calf was in the lead, then came Jean. I brought up the rear on a red yearling heifer that could throw the hair off her back.

I was holding on like a lean tick to a dog's ear and they all came around like a cyclone. As Jess's calf went through the pass way, Jess got his foot caught in the fence. The calf ran out from under him and left him hanging by one leg, his body on the hay in the path of the other calves.

Jean was right behind him; his calf stopped short, but Jean went on top of Jess and the calf ran over both of them.

They were still on the hay when I came along.

My red heifer gave a bellow and threw them both into the fence. She jumped over them, scraping me off on the fence rails as she went.

Then all the other calves in the lot came on around and ran over us.

We were a badly skinned-up bunch when we finally got out of there and climbed on the fence and looked at ourselves.

We went back to the straw stack and tried to clean up a little before Mother saw us.

About that time Jess Hymer's two brothers, John and Jim, another neighbor boy, John Stewart, and Dempsey Gillstrap rode up.

John Stewart was selling my stepfather some cattle and had come to get him.

My stepfather had a little old Indian saddle with only one cinch and I told him he could use my saddle.

After the two of them had gone we got to talking about riding and planned for each of us to saddle and ride a steer.

There was a longhorn spotted steer in the bunch and it fell to me to ride him.

He was easy to catch for he would go out of his way to fight a man.

We got a rope on him, drew him up to the fence and put the old Indian saddle on him. It didn't stick very well so I put my horsehair rope around it and across the saddle scat three times, drew it up tight and piled on him.

Now, that hair rope was double-sheared and it was like sitting on a dozen rows of sharp pinpoints and I saw at once that I had made a big mistake.

When I hit that saddle the old steer started bucking; I stayed until he hit me three times with that rope and then tried to get behind the saddle but I couldn't make it. I let all holds go and went over the steer's head. I landed on my hands and knees and the steer hit me and knocked me about ten feet. That time I landed on my back.

As the steer came in again I kicked him in the nose with my spurs and Jean got him by the tail.

38

Then he took after Jean, who climbed the fence, so the steer turned back to me and I got up on the straw stack just ahead of him.

Jim Hymer roped the steer and he and John Dempsey drew him up to the fence and took off the rope and saddle.

John thought he could ride the longhorn so he put his own saddle on him and crawled on and they turned him loose.

The steer made a few circles around the straw stack, then ran across the lot and jumped the fence.

Dempsey was thrown over the top rail while the steer went pitching off into the timber with Dempsey's stirrups flying over his back at every plunge.

We spent the rest of the day roping him and getting Dempsey's saddle back again.

Our Sunday clothes looked terrible but my stepfather and John Stewart came in about an hour before sundown with about one hundred head of cattle my stepfather had bought.

They had to be cut out and put in the branding lot to be branded with the Goodhue brand, so we all helped and that gave us an excuse for our torn and dirty clothes.

Mother never knew how we had spent our day of rest.

THE PANTHER

One day while Jean and I were hunting, we jumped a large panther. The dogs ran him into a cave about a mile from the house. We could not see him, for the entrance was crooked. We could not afford to waste powder shooting at random, so we rolled some rocks down in the mouth of the cave, shut it up tight, and went home and told our stepfather.

He went back to the cave with us and plugged up the hole a little better and told us to hunt in some other place.

In about ten days an Indian boy named Dave Reed came to visit us and we told him of the big cat in the cave.

He told us he would give us a whole tanned buckskin for the teeth and claws to make a necklace. We waited until he had gone, got our dogs and guns and, telling our stepfather our intentions, struck out for the cave.

We started rolling the rocks away and the dogs began barking.

After some time we got the entrance clear and the panther came charging out. He sure was mad!

He ripped Jean's pants-leg completely off with one blow of his paw.

The dogs came on in and he killed one of them and hurt both the others before we killed him. We shot him four times before we got him down.

In the midst of the fight my stepfather came running up but didn't fire a shot.

After it was all over, he went into the cave and found the big cat had killed a deer and had it in the cave when he was shut in; that was what had kept him alive so long.

My son took me back there last summer and I found the cave where we killed the panther.

The old hills of our old hunting grounds are just as they used to be seventy-five years ago! I am the only thing that has changed and run down to nothing. But it is all right, and as it should be, or it would not have happened. Nature knows what it is doing because Nature is God.

4 LIGHTNING ON THE DRAW

COUNCIL HOUSE

JESSE Thompson, the Indian my stepfather had leased our land from, was re-elected as councilman for Cooweescoowec District for a fourth term.

There were two factions in the district, one led by Tom Downing, the other by a man named Ross.

There was much bad feeling between them. Jesse was on the Downing side.

There was going to be a meeting at the Dog Creek council house, and Jesse had to be there. Jesse's friend, Mac Jackson, was usually with him everywhere he went; he was a big fellow and a good shot, but this time he couldn't go.

There were a good many Ross men along the road to the council house so Jesse asked my mother and stepfather if I might go along with him. I was now fifteen years old and a pretty good shot.

He gave me a new forty-five Colt revolver and a box of shells. These were no doubt for his own protection but I was very happy. Those were the first shells I ever saw.

As we rode along I killed four wolves and one deer.

We put the deer on behind my saddle and took it down to the council house, where we had a big feed for everyone that night.

Some of the councilors doubted I had killed the deer with a belt gun but Jesse had me do some fancy shooting and they were soon convinced.

JIM STARR

One of the councilmen at the meeting was Big Jim Starr, a full-blooded Cherokee Indian.

He was six feet eight inches tall, weighing over three hundred pounds, and was raw-boned, without an ounce of surplus flesh.

He could ride his pony under the limb of a tree, lock his feet under the pony's belly and lift himself and the pony off the ground with his arms. He was the biggest, strongest man I ever saw.

Jim Starr was the only man who ever made a treaty with a Nation. The Cherokee Nation made a treaty with him that if he would quit fighting they would quit chasing him, and they both lived up to the bargain!

I knew about Big Jim, but this was the first time I ever saw him. He liked me and we were friends. He and Tom Downing gave me another Colt forty-five with two boxes of shells and offered to bet anyone that I could shoot faster and truer than any man at the council meeting.

A few tried and were badly beaten.

None of the Ross men could come anywhere near shooting with me.

I was acclaimed the best shot in Cooweescoowee District, and Jesse Thompson was treated royally all through the council meeting and was elected Speaker and Chairman of the Council for Cooweescoowee District.

Every day I killed squirrels and prairie chickens and they had a big feed in the evening. I made many good friends that were a great help to me in later years.

When the council meeting was over even the Ross men shook hands with me and asked me to come and visit them.

Jesse Thompson and I rode home without mishap and for the first time I realized what I had accomplished in all my years of working to be a good shot.

I thought of all the hours I had spent in practice and was not content to stop but only encouraged to try all the harder. To be ready for the job ahead of me I had to be better than just good!

MY FIRST JOB

In the year 1875, soon after the trip to the council house, I began riding the range and looking after the stock for Osage Brown, a cattleman on Mission Creek in the Osage Nation.

The line between the Osage Nation and the Cherokee Nation was the ninety-sixth meridian; it runs right over the east side of the round mound west of where the city of Bartlesville, Oklahoma, now stands.

One day, while talking to some of the other riders, I learned that Shannon Campsey, one of the men who killed my father, was down on the Canadian River, southwest of Webbers Falls.

So I began laying my plans to pay him a visit.

Before I started out on the trail of the killers, however, I wanted to see if I could learn more about shooting. I kept thinking of what Mose Beaman had said that night my father was shot down in cold blood, "I want you to be good for the job ahead of you or you may not get it all done. You must never stop until they are all accounted for!"

I had a duty to perform and could not afford to miss!

The men I was after were all good shots. I knew I would have to be better than they were, able to shoot faster and truer — and must be quicker on the draw.

FORT GIBSON

There was a garrison of cavalry stationed at Fort Gibson, in the northeast part of the Indian Territory, not far from the Arkansas line.

Among the soldiers were some who were noted for their marksmanship.

I decided to go there and try to learn more about handling a gun, so I made my arrangements and set out on my pony for Fort Gibson.

It took me about a week of easy riding through some of the best land in the world, some timber, some grassland and lots of good farming country.

I arrived at Fort Gibson early in the morning. It was a beautiful place. The buildings were of the native stone and it was on the Grand River, one of the prettiest streams in the country. Farther north, the Neosho River empties into the Grand and about fifty miles south of Fort Gibson, the Grand flows into the Arkansas River.

Steamboats called "the little steamers" used to come up the river in the early days carrying supplies for the fort and some passengers.

There were about five hundred men stationed at Fort Gibson at that time and they wore the regulation cavalry uniform, blue pants with yellow stripes down the side and a blue blouse with brass buttons and yellow trimming.

COLONEL COPINGER

As I came up the road in sight of the fort I was accosted by a soldier who asked my business there. "I want to see the commanding officer," I replied, and another soldier standing nearby took me to Colonel Copinger, the commanding officer of the fort.

The colonel was sitting on the gallery, at the headquarters building. He looked me over and asked in his kind, friendly manner, "Well, son, what do you want?"

"I have heard that you have in your command the best and fastest shots in the Territory and I came here to see if they would show me some of their shooting and maybe teach me a few things," I told him.

"You have two guns and you ought to know how to use them."

"That is why I came here: to be able to use them with the best of them."

"Who are you, son?" he asked.

"My name is Frank Eaton. I am a stepson of J. N. Goodhue, who was a soldier in the Thirty-second Iowa Infantry.

My father, Frank Eaton, was in Stannard's Vermont Regiment. His brother, my uncle, was killed at Gettysburg."

I was hoping he would not ask me why I was so anxious to learn more about shooting.

"You are too young to join the army now."

He thought I wanted to join the army? Well, that was just fine!

"I know," I said, "but if I am an expert with my guns I will make a better soldier when I do join, if I ever do. Please let me stay and learn all your men can teach me."

"All right, son," he said, "how did you come here?"

"Horseback," I replied.

Turning to a soldier sitting near him, the colonel said, "Sergeant, take the boy and his pony down to the stables; have him unsaddle and feed his mount and put him in the stall. Then bring the boy back here. I want to talk with him further."

After putting my horse away, rubbing him down and feeding him some hay, we went back to Colonel Copinger.

I was then subjected to a lengthy session of questioning but I gave all the answers straight and true, omitting only my reason for wanting proficiency in gun work.

That afternoon the colonel and a group of soldiers took me to the rifle range and the officer was genuinely surprised at my skill with my guns. I beat them all with the belt guns although they out-shot me with the rifle.

In spite of the grim task that had been set before me I was always of a lighthearted, happy disposition. I made friends easily, so I was soon on friendly terms with all the soldiers at the fort.

Colonel Copinger invited me to supper.

At the table he poured out a glass of wine for each of the men and offered one to me. I told him I had promised my mother that I would never drink any kind of intoxicating liquor until I was forty years old. She said by that time I would know what it would do to me and I could use my own judgment.

I didn't tell him of the promise I had made to Mose Beaman, not to drink a drop until the last Ferber and the last Campsey were accounted for!

Colonel Copinger was pleased and all the men encouraged me in my good resolution.

The meal passed pleasantly.

After supper we all went out on the gallery and talked. I sang the old cowboy songs and told them about my home and of my riding for Osage Brown, how Jesse Thompson had given me one of my guns, and Tom Downing and Big Jim Starr had given me the other one, but the holster and belt I had always had.

"I knew you were no novice with shooting irons," said Colonel Copinger.

I looked down at the holster and belt that Mose Beaman had given me so long ago and wished that he could hear what the colonel had said.

"Why is it," asked the sergeant, who was sitting on the edge of the gallery, "that you are so willing to tell us all about yourself? Most of the folks we meet won't even tell us their names."

"Oh," I said, "I am not ashamed of my name. My life is an open book and anyone can read it who wants to and those who like it are my friends, and the ones who don't like it can leave me alone and we will get along anyhow."

They all laughed and after a little while the colonel said, "Tomorrow we will do some more shooting, on foot and on horseback, too, for I want to see how good you really are."

"I will do my best, sir," I said.

The men got up to go to their quarters for the night.

They offered me a bunk but I told them I would rather sleep on the grass. I understood the grass but I had never seen an army bunk before.

The next day we had more matches.

I out shot them again with the pistols, but again they beat me with the rifles. My Winchester did not have the range their Springfield's had, nor the shock and penetration.

After the shooting matches we ran horse races, footraces, had jumping and wrestling matches, pitched horse- shoes and had a lot of fun.

THE OLD SCOUT'S DRAW

There was an old scout named Busby who didn't talk much but showed a keen interest in all that took place.

That evening as I was singing and cleaning my guns the old man came and sat down on the ground beside me.

"I have been watching you," he said, "and there is something I think I can show you. It is the underhand draw.

You already have the knack of pointing your gun at the target without sighting. If you can get this draw as fast as your straight draw you will be a hard kid to beat. It is done this way." And he put on one of my guns and showed

me how it was done. I watched him closely.

He showed me the few moves involved; then, handing me the belt and gun, told me to try it.

I did, and on the second attempt made a perfect draw.

"I knew it," said the old scout, "I knew you could learn quick. Now, son, keep practicing and you will be faster than Wild Bill and he is plenty fast."

The old scout went on his way to the stable but I kept working on that draw.

When I went to bed I lay there trying to figure out a still faster way until I dropped off to sleep. And then I dreamed that I had found it!

Next morning I tried it just as I had dreamed and sure enough it was a shade faster!

After breakfast Colonel Copinger came out with a marksmanship badge; pinning it on me, he said, "I am giving you this badge for your fine marksmanship and I am going to give you a new name.

From now on you are Pistol Pete! What do you think of that?"

"It's all right with me." And I thanked him for a fine time and a good name. "If I ever enlist I want to be in your command," I told him; and I meant it.

"I hope you may be," said the colonel, "and if I can ever be of any help let me know; I will do all I can for you."

Thanking him again, I went down to the stables to get my pony and there I met the old scout, Busby, coming out of the door.

Well, good-by, son," he said, "be careful and keep practicing that draw that I showed you."

"I will. And look here." I threw my gun with the new twist I had learned from my dream.

The old scout looked at me in surprise. "Do that again, son, you were too fast for me that time." I tried to be even faster than before.

He shook his head.

"Son," he said, "you are a wonder! I have seen some of the fastest men in the country and you sure have them shaded. But don't get careless and get rusty or some damn fool will out live you."

49

He went on toward the barracks and I saddled my pony and went up to headquarters to tell the boys good-by

A GOOD STUNT

I left Fort Gibson feeling able to take care of myself in most any kind of crowd, and determined to master the new draw.

Before long I was pretty good, and the time came when I was fast as lightning.

There are people who still remember a stunt I used to do. This is the way it was done: A four-inch target was placed at twenty feet on an anvil block. A steel disk off a disk plow, or a piece of steel that would ring, was placed on the floor.

I stood, with my gun loose in the holster, both hands extended straight out in front of me, directly over the steel disk. A five-eighths metal washer was placed on the back of one hand. With my hands straight out in front of me, backs up, I turned my hands slowly until the washer began to slide.

When the washer slid I drew my gun and fired. The report of the gun came before the ring of the washer hitting the metal disk on the floor. The trick was to hit the bull's-eye every time.

5 ON THE TRAIL

THE TOTEM

WHEN I left Fort Gibson, I rode slowly, making inquiries along the way. By the time I reached home I was fairly well informed as to the whereabouts of Shannon Campsey.

I let my pony rest for a few days while I worked on my outfit and got everything ready.

This was the beginning of the job I had been preparing myself to do for so many years. That was the year 1876.

Early one morning I started out for Webbers Falls. My brother rode with me for a little way. It was a beautiful morning. The birds were singing and the tall grass was green and fragrant.

As we rode up to Jesse Thompson's place, his wife, Granny Thompson, came out and waited for me at the side of the path.

In her hand she carried a small piece of buckskin. It was about three inches wide and about one foot long and on it there were some queer-shaped marks. They were Indian symbols burned into the buckskin with the heated point of a knife dipped in tattoo ink.

Pointing to the marks, the old woman said: "There is a man named Jim Childers, who has a ferry on the Arkansas River just above Broken Arrow.

He is a Cherokee Indian like me. When you get there, show him this totem and he will tell you all you want to know of the people in that part of the Nation, where to stay at night among friends and who to go to for help — if you need help. Now, my boy, may God bless you and bring you safe home to us again."

I thanked her, put the totem in my gun belt and rode on, wondering how she knew where I was going and if she guessed the purpose of my errand.

Jean rode with me to the south end of Nigger-gap, then he cut across the hills to try to kill a deer on the way home.

I rode on alone.

This was the beginning of a mission that could end only one-way: when the Campseys and the Ferbers were "all accounted for"!

I rode on down by L. Taota's and passed Pete Perrier's.

I crossed Bird Creek at Bill Rogers's store, where the town of Skiatook, Oklahoma, now stands.

I stopped at Burt Norton's Ranch and Trail Supplies, a store that sold everything. This store was located where the city of Tulsa is today. At that time, in addition to the store there was a blacksmith shop and four or five dwellings. I bought some canned goods and another box of shells for my rifle and went on down the river.

There were a few farms in the bottoms and the whole country abounded in hogs, cattle and horses.

JIM CHILDERS

When I got to the ferry on the Arkansas River the boat was on the other side.

The ferryman was up at the house after a drink of water, but he came when he heard my hail.

As we ferried back across the river I asked him if his name was Jim Childers. He said it was and I took out the piece of buckskin and handed it to him. He looked at the marks and said, "So you are a friend of Jesse Thompson and therefore a friend of mine and the Downings.

You must stay all night with us. Take your pony out and we will talk after I tell the woman."

He went into the house with the totem in his hand.

I took the saddle and bridle off my pony and tied him where he could get lots of grass without getting tangled up in the brush. Then I hung my trappings up on the porch beside those of Childers and went into the house.

"This is my wife," said Jim, "she will put some more marks on your totem before you leave in the morning. Now we will go down to the boat and talk."

Sitting on a log in the shade of a tree Jim asked me why I was looking for Shannon Campsey.

So Granny Thompson had known, and had put it on the totem!

"You cannot be my friend and his, too," he said, "for he steals the Indians' cattle and ponies. He drives them up across the Arkansas River and someone meets him there and he drives them on up to the Illinois River. Then an-other man meets the herd there and drives them up into the States and sells them. The Indians get nothing."

I told him the whole story, how the Campseys and the Ferbers had killed my father when I was only eight years old, of the years I had spent since then learning to shoot and waiting to get old enough to bring them to justice.

Now I was almost sixteen years old and I was on the trail of the whole gang; I intended to clean them all out before I stopped.

Jim Childers listened earnestly to my story and when I had finished he said: "Big Jim Starr told me about you a long time ago, the time you went down to the Dog Creek council house with Jesse Thompson for the council meeting. He told me about your shooting. If we had known about this we would have come after you and then they would not have stolen any more ponies from us. But now you come; we will help, and maybe we get all of them."

I told him that all the help I wanted was to find them. I would do the rest myself; I didn't want anything to happen to them now, until I got through with my job.

Jim's wife had come out in time to hear my story. She went into the house and got her tattoo ink and a sharp piece of wood and began marking on the piece of buckskin. She took lots of pains to make the marks just in a certain shape and position.

After she had finished she examined it closely from every angle, then handed it to me, saying; "You take it now and Jim will tell you in the morning."

Thanking her, I put the buckskin back in my gun belt and Jim and I sat and talked.

Just before sundown two men came up and wanted to cross the ferry. I rode over with them and could tell that Jim did not like them.

As soon as they led their ponies off the boat Jim took in his lines and set the boat to go back across the river, while the two men mounted and rode away.

After they were out of hearing Jim said, "They are bad Indians. They help Shannon Campsey steal ponies. I sure am glad you are going to kill him before he gets a chance to steal any more ponies. You will get there day after tomorrow and then Shannon Campsey will stop stealing ponies for good."

54

The next morning, as I was coiling my rope, Jim's wife came out to where Jim and I were standing. She put a large corn pone and some fried bacon in my saddle pockets.

"When you get to Reed and Palone's Camp," she said, "go to see Emiline Palone and tell her I am all right, for she is my sister. Show that totem to Andy Reed and he will tell you where to find Shan Campsey."

I thanked her and, after shaking hands with Jim, mounted and was on my way.

Jim had told me all about the trails and how to reach Reed and Palone's, who were all living in the same camp.

The next morning I arrived at the camp and was taken to Andy Reed's place.

I showed him the buckskin and told him what Jim and his wife had said. He looked at the totem and then at me and finally he said; "You are too much of a boy yet to fight that bunch. I will take some of my men and go with you."

"No," I protested, "just tell me where he lives and how to get there and I will do the rest. I may be just a boy but I know how to fight such dirty skunks as they are."

"Well," he said, "you stay and eat dinner and I will tell you all you want to know while we eat."

After dinner I was getting ready to leave when I saw a small group of men on their ponies and noticed they were all heavily armed.

"Now see here," I cried, "this is my fight and I want to do it in my way."

"That's all right," said Andy Reed, "these men are going to wait at the spring on the other side of Shan Campsey's house. If you get hurt they will take care of you. They won't fight till you get done fighting. So after you leave Shan's house go around the yard fence and take the path to the spring, where we will be waiting for you."

SHANNON CAMPSEY

This was my first fight and I was eager to get it over with, so I rode at a fox trot for about five miles. I took the trail he had told me. It led up the big hill, then around the hill to another trail, then up the draw.

Coming around the point of the hill I saw the one-room log house where Shannon Campsey lived, about a half mile ahead in a clearing, at the head of the draw near a little branch. It was daubed with mud on the outside.

There was a high paling fence surrounding the house and it had a porch made of logs across the front. Shan could sit up there and look down and see who was coming up the trail.

As I approached I saw Shannon Campsey get up and go into the house and come out with a Winchester.

He sat down in the chair with the Winchester across his lap and watched me.

I knew he was fast and a dead shot. But I had been trained for this since I was eight years old, since the night when Shannon Campsey had emptied his gun into my father's body as he lay dead at his feet, and then had kicked me and struck me with his whip.

I rode up to the fence, which was about thirty feet from the house.

Getting off my horse, I called out, "Hello, Shan, don't you know me?"

At the sound of his name Shan jumped to his feet and raised his rifle to fire, but he was too slow. Like a rattler striking, my hand went to my hip.

Before Shan's gun went off there were two forty-fives through his breast.

He fell on his face on the ground with his gun under him.

56

I got on my horse with my gun still in my hand, looking sharply for other foes. I rode around the house and took the trail to the spring. Halfway there I met Andy Reed and his men riding up the trail to meet me.

"We heard two shots just like one," he said. "We thought he had shot you."

"No," I said, "I fired twice to be sure."

"How the hell you shoot so fast?" asked Andy.

"Oh, that's easy when you know how," I said and fired two shots at a knot in a tree putting both fairly in the center of the knot. Then reloading my gun I stuck it back into the holster.

"Give me your totem," said Andy.

He had brought some tattoo ink to fix my totem and with his knife he put some symbols on it and gave it back to me.

"Now," he said, "you go back to the ferry. Give this to Jim Childers and he will tell you what to do. We will wait here for a while so that if any of this gang try to follow you we can stop them."

As I rode away I saw them conceal themselves in the brush along the trail while one of them took the ponies around the bend out of sight.

I rode all night that night, and the next evening, as I came in sight of the ferry, Jim Childers came up from the boat to meet me. "Hello," he said, "back so soon? Did you find your man?"

I handed him the totem and he took it into the house and showed it to his wife.

I staked my pony and hung up my saddle and while the woman got supper I told them the story.

After I had finished Jim said, "Yes, that is what Andy told me on the totem. Now, what are you going to do?"

"There is a whole gang of them," I said. "I think about all the men I want are in it. I am going to keep going until I find out for sure and if they are, I won't have so much country to ride over."

"That's right," said Jim, "and now you go to Big Jim Starr. He knows about them; he has his men watching and he will help you find them. When you get through come back and stay with us and we will treat you good."

I promised that if I came out all right I would come back and visit them. Then I got my blanket and went to bed on the gallery, with my guns under my head, much to Jim's approval.

The next morning as I led my pony off the ferryboat Jim went up the bank with me and told me how to get to Big Jim Starr's place. He gave me minute directions, telling all about the trails, the streams and the timber.

When I came to the bend in the trail I looked back and saw Jim Childers still standing there watching to see that I took the right trail. I waved my hat and after getting Jim's answer I rode on out of sight of the ferry.

I camped that night and made supper and breakfast on the food Jim's wife had given me.

Early in the morning I started on again, intending to get to the Starr or Downing neighborhood that night.

About an hour by sun — that is, an hour before sundown, I noticed a rider, about half a mile to my left, riding on a line in the same direction as my own.

I rode on for a while, and then turned to intercept him at the edge of the timber.

The rider gave no indication that he noticed the ch~
until we met. He was an Indian and he rode up and a
going.

"I am going to Big Jim Starr's place. Am I on the right trail?"

"Yes, you are on the right trail. What do you want of Big Jim?"

"Andy Reed and Jim Childers told me to go to him," I said.

"Huh, good enough," he said, "you friend of his?"

For answer I took out the totem and handed it to him He looked at it for
a long time. Handing it back to me he said, "Just a boy, killum one man
and want more. Long time ago you come to Council House with Jesse
Thompson. Big Jim tellum how you shootum fast and hitum all the time.
Come, I am Big Jim's kinfolks, I take you home to him," and he led the
way at a lope.

In a short time we reached a big clearing and I saw my old friend, Big Jim
Starr, coming to meet me.

I jumped off my pony and we shook hands warmly. I staked my horse
and hung up my saddle.

We went outside to where the man who had brought me in was talking to
a group of men in their own language.

The men were all Indians and I could not understand them. Then Big Jim
Starr started talking to them in Cherokee. They listened until he had
finished. Then they all came and shook my hand.

I gave Big Jim the totem and he looked at the symbols and began talking
again. Then they all talked and at the conclusion of the talk they all came
and shook my hand again in a most friendly manner.

e boy, killum horse thief, going to getum all. Good, we will all help
n you get ready," they said.

thanked them, but told them I only wanted them to tell me where the
men were and I would do the rest.

"Just like you did at Andy Reed's place," said Big Jim, smiling at me. "I
knew a long time ago that you were good and I would not want you on
my trail."

The other men all grunted their approval of what Big Jim said and started
talking out their plans for the elimination of the gang of horse thieves.

I told them of the two men who crossed the ferry and they looked at
each other and grinned, their white teeth gleaming against their smooth
dark skins.

"Yes, we know about them," said Big Jim,

"Captain Sam Sixkiller got them yesterday. He is up in Going Snake
District but will be back pretty soon, maybe in time to help us. I want
you to see him so you will know him, for he is like you, good quick shot,
hot-blooded. It would be too bad for you and him not to know one
another for you might not understand and fight. Then we lose two good
men at the same time!"

6 THE LIGHTHORSE

CAPTAIN SAM SIXKILLER

THE Lighthorse was like the Mounted Police.

In the Indian Territory, in those days, each of the Nations had its own Lighthorse. They rode everywhere and in their own Nation had absolute authority. They worked with the United States Marshals and were groups of Cherokees, Creeks and Seminoles.

The Lighthorse were all Indians, belonging to the tribe in the Nation where they rode. They were picked men, the best shots in the country; they carried the best equipment, rode the best horses, were always there when needed and were not afraid of man or devil.

When a man the Lighthorse was after crossed into another Nation, they rode with the Lighthorsemen of that Nation to hunt for him.

There was no such thing as a man getting away from the Lighthorse if he stayed in the Indian Territory — and if he crossed the Red River into Texas, the Texas Rangers got him.

Captain Sam Sixkiller was in command of the Lighthorse in the Cherokee Nation.

A couple of days after I arrived at Big Jim Starr's place, Captain Sixkiller came in from his trip to Going Snake District and he and Big Jim had a long talk. Afterwards they came out where I was jumping and wrestling with the young Indians.

Captain Sam Sixkiller was a full-blooded Cherokee Indian and as fine a specimen of manhood as you could find in a day's ride.

He was about six feet tall, with broad shoulders and a slim waist, with heavy limbs and joints, and the lithe and sinewy actions of a panther. He weighed one hundred and eighty pounds and was a fine looking man, with regular features, a frank, open countenance and a good firm chin. I was glad he was coming as a friend.

We shook hands and looked each other in the eye.

The captain said, "I am glad to meet you, Pistol Pete. Big Jim Starr has told me about you and so has Colonel Copinger at Fort Gibson. We are glad to have you help us in stamping out the cattle thievery going on around here."

"I am glad to be of any help I can," I said.

"The main bunch of them is in Southwest City," said the captain, "and they probably have another place in the hills in Missouri. We have crippled them badly at this end. I think if you go to Bill Downing he can tell you where nearly all the men you want are located. They all belong to this outfit and are a hard bunch to handle. You had better let me go along with you, for you may run into two or three of them at one time."

"I hope I do," I said, "for that will save me a lot of riding."

The captain looked at Big Jim and smiled. Then he said to me, "Now, if you happen to need another horse, just go to Bill Downing or Edgar Halfmoon and show them that piece of buckskin you carry and they will give you one. If you are farther up, go to John Swanick on California

Creek and he will fit you out. Swanick has some good stock and they are fast but he has to watch them close to keep them from being stolen. Now let us figure out our next moves so we will not get in each other's way. Jim tells me you always want to play a lone hand."

We talked and made our plans the rest of the forenoon. After dinner the captain and I had a shooting match and I won!

The captain slapped me on the back and said, "You don't need to be afraid of any of that crowd as long as they are in front of you. But keep a close watch, for any of them would rather shoot at your back."

The next morning I started on. I was in no hurry so took my time. The next afternoon I met an Indian Lighthorseman who turned out to be Bill Downing.

Bill was a cousin of Tom Downing, the councilman at Dog Creek council house who, with Big Jim Starr, had given me the forty-five.

I showed him the totem and he looked at it carefully. Handing it back to me he said, "I am sure glad you came. There are some of your men here now. They have a bunch of stolen cattle, about twenty-five or thirty head, and are driving them away to brand them. When you find their trail you can follow them, but if you should find the men themselves wait for us. I am going after Captain Sam Sixkiller and some of the other boys." And he rode away at a gallop.

DOC FERBER

I rode on and found the trail and followed it to the timber. There, looking back over the prairie, I thought what a fine place it would be for someone to hide and shoot anyone following the trail.

I rode out a few hundred yards from the trail and then started back across.

If anyone was watching the trail they would think I had just crossed and gone on. I rode as if I was not at all suspicious of an ambush but gradually angled up to the timber.

When I got to the edge of the timber I saw there was a deep wooded ravine running down into the woods.

The wind brought me the smell of burned hair and hide and I knew there was someone down there branding cattle.

63

As I got to the head of the ravine a horseman rode up to meet me. There was something familiar in the look of him and when, at a distance of about thirty feet, he stopped and hailed me I knew who he was!

"Hello, boy," he said, "what are you doing here, and what do you want?"

"I just want you, Doc Ferber," I said, "and I am sure glad I have found you."

"Who the hell are you anyhow? And how do you know who I am?"

"I am Frank Eaton and I ought to know you, Doc Ferber, for you are one of the men who killed my father. Fill your hand! You son of a bitch!"

We both went for our guns but Doc didn't have a Chinaman's chance. I had been working on that draw for years, just to use at this moment.

Doc went off his horse, headlong to the ground, his gun exploding as he landed stone dead, with two forty-five slugs through his breast.

There were a couple of shots from the ravine and two men started out toward me.

I drew my Winchester from the scabbard and was dismounted and waiting for them.

I heard the sound of running horses, and whirling around saw Captain Sam Sixkiller, Bill Downing and about half a dozen Lighthorsemen as they dashed past me and made for the men who had fired at me.

Jumping on my horse I took out after them.

They had fast horses and I didn't catch them until they were right on the men, who gave up after firing only one or two shots.

The two men were disarmed and their hands tied behind them, with a Lighthorseman leading each of their ponies.

64

They all rode down to the branding lot but there was no one there, only the cattle, the fires and the branding irons.

They looked the cattle over and found four or five different brands, proving they had been stolen from several different herds. Then the Lighthorsemen looked to see what brand the men were putting on the cattle and found it was Doc Ferber's.

"Well," said Captain Sam, "he won't ship them right away, anyhow."

Then turning to me he said, "Say, pardner, you sure got guts! We were watching you and it was worth a lot to see the way you acted. Were you going to stay and fight the other two?"

"Why sure," I said, "one or both of them might have been the men I wanted. Anyhow, they were in damned bad company. Captain, let me talk to them. They might be able to tell me something I want to know."

"Sure," said the captain, "turn your wolf loose; we are in no hurry to hang them. There is plenty of time and they might talk to you better than they would for us. And now, boys," he continued as I walked over to where the two prisoners were sitting on the ground, "he will guard the men and we will burn this damn place and drive the stock out on the range and let them go home. Keep tally on whose brand they wear and we will notify the owners. This was a lucky day for us!"

I squatted down facing the prisoners and started to talk to them. They were sullen and mean and one of them said, "How come you shot Doc Ferber and didn't try to arrest him?"

"I am no officer," I said, "and it was purely a personal matter between Doc and me. Say, fellows, I want to tell you why I am here."

In a few words I told them my story and then concluded, "Now, boys, I have got two of these men who killed my father and I am going to keep on until I get them all. If you know anything that will help me, tell me

65

and maybe I can help you." However, it didn't look like there was much I could do for them.

The two men looked at each other; one of them nodded and the other one said, "Now, son, is that your only reason for following our trail?"

"It is," I said, "and as soon as I finish my job I am going back home and behave myself."

"All right, son," he said, "John Ferber is in Southwest City, Missouri. Jonce and Jim Campsey are out in Douglas County, somewhere near Buckhart, but Wyley Campsey killed a fellow and had to leave the country. We don't know where he went — out in the Southwest someplace, I think, but I'm not sure."

I thanked them and shook hands with them; then, calling a Lighthorseman to watch them, I went to Captain Sixkiller and told him what I had learned from the two men.

"Well," said the captain, "we will camp here tonight and you can start in the morning. I have no authority outside the Cherokee Nation but I am going to Southwest City with you. They all know me there and I can fix it easy for you so no one will bother you."

"That will be fine," I said, "only I want to have a free hand to do as I please and not be hampered too much with interference until I find Wyley Campsey."

Captain Sixkiller laughed and said, "Nothing has bothered you so far."

"Then it is all right with me and I am glad you are going along to fix it up for me."

The next morning, after he gave his orders to his men regarding the prisoners, the captain and I rode off for Southwest City.

We arrived without mishap and put our ponies into the livery barn.

The captain went to police headquarters and I went to the hotel to get our rooms and look around for John Ferber.

I got the rooms and was starting out when I met Captain Sixkiller coming in.

JOHN FERBER

"You are a little too late," the captain said. "John Ferber was killed in a poker game last night when they caught him stealing a card. He is down at the undertaker's right now."

"Let's go down and see if it is really him." I wanted to be sure.

We went down to the undertaker's and sure enough there he lay, with a forty-four clear through him.

"Ain't that hell?" I said. "Here I rode five hundred miles for him and somebody else beat me to him! Well, I will go to his funeral and maybe Jim or Jonce Campsey will be there."

The next morning we were up early and after breakfast we went back to the undertaker's. The place was full of officers watching for some of Ferber's friends who might be wanted by the law.

Captain Sixkiller was talking to a bunch of the officers telling them what I had done and getting their promise to help me break up the rest of the gang.

There was a tall man with light blond hair who listened all the time the captain was talking. After he had finished the tall man got up and came over to where I was standing, looking down at the corpse.

CHRIS ADAMS

"Can I have a few words with you after the funeral?" he asked me.

"Sure you can, then or right now," I said as I looked him over.

"I will wait until after the funeral," he said and he walked over and stood by the window, drumming on the glass with his fingers.

I watched him.

After the funeral was over and we had all come back from Boot Hill the stranger came and asked me to go with him.

"Lead the way," I said and followed him up to his room in the hotel.

Pushing a chair up to the table for me, and sitting down in another one, the stranger looked at me. I was still standing.

Laying both hands on the table, palms down, he said, "Sit down, son, I am a friend and I want you to help me."

"All right," I said and I sat down slowly.

"It's just this," he said, observing my caution and smiling broadly. "I am going to show my hand. My name is Chris Adams and I am a Deputy United States Marshal!"

He showed me his badge and commission. "I have been working on this case for some time. You and I have been after the same men and you have done more in three weeks than I have done in six months."

No! No! That wasn't right! He didn't know the years of work and waiting that were behind me!

A DEPUTY UNITED STATES MARSHAL

Chris Adams, after explaining to me that he had the authority to appoint anyone he wanted to help him, offered me a Deputy United States Marshal's commission.

He said he would turn over to me the case involving the men I was after, and I could work it out in my own way with a free hand and the authority to do as I pleased.

68

This was more than I had ever dreamed of. I accepted, saying, "All right and I will do my damnedest to be worthy of the trust you give me."

Adams reached for his hat and said, "Let's go down to headquarters."

We entered the building and went over to Judge Charles Bailey's desk. Chris Adams spoke to him. "Judge, I want you to swear this boy in as a Deputy United States Marshal. I am giving him charge of the job I have been on."

"I am glad to do it," said the judge. "Captain Sam Sixkiller has told me about him and he is capable of doing a man's part anywhere."

He told me to raise my right hand and he swore me in as a Deputy United States Marshal for the Western District of Arkansas, presided over by Judge Isaac C. Parker, at Fort Smith, Arkansas, where the old Federal Jail was located.

As Chris Adams gave me my badge and commission he said, "Now, son, you can wear this badge or carry it in your pocket, but always have it with you; you may need to show it to some of the officers in the towns you visit. May your good luck continue forever!" He shook my hand.

Federal Jail Fort Smith Arkansas

Adams then gave me all the information he had concerning the whereabouts of Jonce and Jim Campsey, and the local officers promised him to give me all the help I needed.

Before leaving, he told me to be sure to look him up when I went to Fort Smith, saying I could find him through Judge Isaac C. Parker, who always knew where he was.

That was the year 1877. I was seventeen years old too young to be a Deputy United States Marshal; but my case was an exception.

In those days the average length of a marshal's life was about eighteen months.

During the time I "rode for Parker" in a space of six to eight years, sixty-five officers of the Fort Smith Court were killed. Over half of them were under thirty-five years of age.

There was little respect for the law in those days and in most places the law enforcement officers were regarded as interfering with the rights of other people.

7 STOLEN CATTLE AND DEAD MEN

RIDING back into the hills again, I saw a good many cattle.

In one bunch there was about a dozen with the brand of Hooley Bell, a Cherokee Indian stockman. I began to look around then, and found the brands of Alex Adair, the Owens Cattle Company, Clem Rogers and a preacher by the name of Charlie Journeycake, all men I knew.

After thinking it over I went back to Southwest City and wrote a letter to Captain Sam Sixkiller, one to Bill Downing and another to Clem Rogers, telling them what I had seen.

THE TWO CAMPSEYS

The next morning I started out again.

I rode steadily all morning; and that afternoon, as I came out into a clearing, not far away I saw a house near a spring, on the side of a hill. I rode up and hailed a man who was sitting by the side of the house. He got up and came toward me and I asked for a drink of water and if I could stay all night.

He was a native and a typical backwoodsman. "Where you from?" he asked.

I had a good story ready. "I am from Claremore," I replied.

"What are you doing up here?"

"My father has lost a few cattle and I am looking for them. I see quite a few head of cattle around here. Who do they belong to and where is their ranch?"

"They belong to Jim and Jonce Campsey, and their place is a right smart ways from here," said the man. "Now tie your hoss to the fence and when the boy comes in I think we can put you up for the night."

I tied my pony and went and sat on the bench beside the old man and we talked until about an hour by sun.

Then the boy came around the house. He was about twenty-five years old and carried a long rifle, a powder horn and a bullet pouch.

"Hello, stranger, what are you after?" he asked.

I told him the story I had told his father about looking for my father's cattle and asked to stay all night.

I could see him turning my story over in his mind and I had another thought. "If I find any of the cattle I will have to have help to get them out of the timber. Could I hire you to help me? I will pay you well if you will help me drive them as far as Southwest City. But I have not found any of them yet."

That did it!

"If I were you," said the boy, "I would go to Jim and Jonce Campsey. They are all the time riding around and if your cattle are here they will know it. Then I will help you drive them to town."

I stayed there all night and in the morning the boy told me how to find the place where Jim and Jonce Campsey lived.

After breakfast I started out and rode at a steady gait. Before noon I was in sight of the house where the two men lived.

After all these years I was about to come face to face again with two of the men who had killed my father, probably both at the same time. What would be the end?

72

Was I good enough to handle both of them?

I could hear Mose Beaman's words, "You must never stop until they are all accounted for."

If I came through this, there was only one more, Wyley Campsey!

As I rode up to the fence Jonce was at the wash bench washing his hands. Jim was not in sight and I wondered where he was. I didn't want him coming up behind me.

"Is this where Jim and Jonce Campsey live?" I asked Jonce.

"It is," he said.

"Are you Jim Campsey?" I asked. I knew he was not but thought it a good way to find out where Jim was.

"No, I am Jonce."

"Well, I have a message for no one but Jim. I was told not to give it to anyone else."

"Who gave you the message?" asked Jonce.

"Doc Ferber!"

Jim came out of the house with his rifle in his hand.

"I am Jim," he said, "what did Doc say for you to tell me?"

I got off my horse and walked over to the fence, taking my time.

Then I said deliberately, "The game is up. Frank Eaton is going to kill you both. Fill your hands"

They were both in front of me and I could watch every move they made.

I saw Jonce reach for his gun. Then Jim swung his rifle around but he didn't have time to fire it and Jonce's gun shot into the ground as he fell.

MY REPORT

I went back to Southwest City and reported to Judge Bailey — Chris Adams was there, too.

I told them about the stolen cattle and about finding Jim and Jonce with the cattle; that there had been a fight and that the Campseys had come out second best.

The judge just smiled and asked where it all took place.

I told him and he said, "Get some grub and get ready to go with my men and show them what you have told me. The livery man will take care of your horse and let you have a fresh one."

After eating I went down to the livery barn.

The officers were already there. They had a good horse with my saddle on him and were ready to go.

As we passed through the herds of cattle I showed them the different brands and told them whom they belonged to and where they lived.

It was late that evening when we came to the house where the Campseys had lived.

The bodies were lying just as I had left them.

The officers saw that both of the men had weapons and they found the empty shell in Jonce's gun.

They saw where I stood when I fired my gun and the empty shells at the spot. The leader said, "I guess you told it right, son; I would give a lot to have seen it!

Captain Sam Sixkiller was right when he said you packed the fastest guns in the Indian Territory."

Then he turned to his men and said, "Now, boys, we will look in the house for stolen goods. Then we will put these two fellows in the house and set it on fire and save burying them."

In the house they found a lot of loot that had been stolen in the robbery of a store in Baxter Springs, Kansas. Moving it all outside they got the house ready and dragged the dead men inside.

Then they set the house on fire.

"That saves a hell of a lot of digging," said the officer in charge. "Now when we hear from Captain Sixkiller we will get an outfit and round up the stolen cattle and the owners can come and get them."

They packed the stuff they had taken out of the house on their ponies, and started for Southwest City.

We had not gone far when some of the natives came out to meet us holding their guns right on us. They thought we were revenue officers. After finding out who the officers were and what they had done, the natives brought out their moonshine and they all had a drink together and parted friends.

EXONERATED

When the officer in charge of the trip made his report to Judge Bailey, Chris Adams listened closely.

He told them that both of the outlaws were armed, that Jonce had fired one shot from his gun and was lying with the gun still in his hand, that I had not gone inside the fence but had turned and got on my horse and left.

They agreed it was justifiable homicide and told me there was nothing against me.

They both complimented me on the successful termination of the case and asked me to wait and help Captain Sixkiller gather the stolen cattle.

"But, Judge," I protested, "it is costing me like hell to put up at that hotel and keep my pony in the livery barn. I am running out of money and we don't know when Captain Sixkiller will get in."

"Oh, that is all right," said the judge, "we will feed you and your horse till you get ready to leave and it won't cost you a cent for you have more than paid for all we can do for you. I will see the hotelkeeper and the livery stable man and fix it up for you. You have been pretty busy lately and a little rest won't hurt you. Just lie around and enjoy yourself."

I went down to the hotel and went to sleep for the rest of that day and night.

CUTTING OUT STOLEN CATTLE

In a few days Captain Sam Sixkiller and Bill Downing arrived with a chuck wagon and five men to gather the stolen cattle.

After lying in supplies we drove out and made camp, and the real work began.

Captain Sixkiller hired some of the native settlers and got some of the ranchers to help.

We started in at the far end and drove the cattle toward the camp.

They were all Indian cattle, longhorns, and they were scattered in the hills, through the timber and on the prairie. There were brands from all the well-known ranches and from the smaller ones too — brands I was familiar with and some I'd never seen before.

The men split up in threes and fours and took the ravines, the water holes, the timber and the plains and they all drove their cattle to the mouth of the creek.

We met in the evenings. Every rider had five horses and the wrangler always had a fresh horse ready for him.

At night we just dropped the reins, grabbed some beef and sourdough biscuits and went to sleep. Our blankets were spread on the ground with our horses tied to a picket pin at our head. We slept with our hats and boots on, our belts buckled with our guns in the holsters, and our hands on our guns!

In a few days we had all the cattle and horses we could find thrown together.

Word was spread by the Lighthorse that we were driving stolen cattle in to Vinita so that the ranchers from the other parts of the country could meet us there and drive their cattle home.

We cut out all the Indian Territory brands and were ready to drive the rest of the stock to the roundup grounds at Vinita.

UNBROKEN MULES

They had a pair of wild unbroken mules hitched to the chuck wagon and it took the whole outfit to unhitch them or hitch them up again.

Each mule had a long rope tied to the hackamore and running back to the wagon where the driver could reach it.

A hackamore is a rope halter twisted out of a lariat. It went around the mule's nose and ears like the brow band of a bridle. It could be twisted so tight the mule couldn't get his head down.

The mules didn't know what the lines were for and their mouths were tough anyway, so when the driver wanted to turn the team, his helper held one of the mules back by pulling on the rope that was tied to the hackamore while the other mule ran around him.

There were about three hundred head of all kinds of cattle and they were restless and hard to handle.

But the mules ran off with the chuck wagon the first day out and we drove the cattle until we caught up with them.

When we did catch them the cattle were so tired we had them fairly well in hand and after a couple of days they were trail broke and we could manage them.

SOME BRANDS

It was about thirty-five miles to the first ranch, the C (C Bar), where we cut out a few cattle.

The C had cattle all over the country in those days but the cattle thief could be particular; he took only the best and got them as easily as possible.

The next ranch was the PVP about twenty-five miles further on. We cut out about ten or fifteen head there and went on to the J (Bar J), which belonged to the preacher, Charlie Journeycake.

We were getting nearer home now and there were more of the cattle to cut out.

From Charlie Journeycake's ranch we drove the rest of the herd on to Vinita where the owners all rode in to cut out their own cattle and drive them to their home range.

The days were spent on the trail. At night we spread our blanket and slept with our hats on and our guns ready.

Some days we made as much as twenty-five miles and some not more than ten.

I went on to Vinita with the herd and then helped the Owens Cattle Company drive their cattle home.

When we arrived at the Owens Ranch the foreman offered me top hand wages but I was getting homesick and wasn't far from home now — so, telling him I would come back later, I rode on.

It was early spring and there was much work to be done at home and I knew they would need my help. When I arrived home the family was well.

Already they had the teams plowing and I was there in time to help them plow and fence a forty-acre field for a man, named Jasper Exendine, who had been talking to my mother and stepfather about adopting me as his own son

8 THE MATERIAL AT HAND

JASPER EXENDINE

JASPER Exendine was a wonderful man!

You know we used to admire a real man . . . true physical manhood. He was one of the most perfect specimens I ever knew. Six feet three and one-half inches tall, he weighed about two hundred twenty-five pounds, pure brawn and muscle.

He had a thick black mustache but was bald when I first knew him, black eyes that looked right through you but were still very kind.

He had a good-shaped head with a prominent forehead. His head was sort of square and well set on his thick neck and heavy shoulders.

He was a happy-go-lucky fellow, but his word was as good as his bond.

Jasper was part Cherokee Indian and his wife was a full-blooded Delaware. They had no children at that time and had always been very fond of me. They had always wanted me for their own son and now my mother and stepfather were willing for them to adopt me legally.

Later Jasper and his wife raised a large family of their own. One of their sons, Albert Exendine, was a famous football star at Carlisle Indian School, and was later back field coach at A. and M. College, Stillwater, Oklahoma.

He was there for a long time before he went into the Indian Service in Oklahoma City where he still is.

Jasper was one Indian who never drank whisky, but he used to drink beer sometimes. At times he played drink-or-smell. You don't know what that is? Well, that's when you play poker: if you win you drink; if you lose you smell the winners' breath! But that was beer, not whisky!

SPORTS

Jasper Exendine excelled at all kinds of sports, running, jumping and wrestling.

None of the boys around our parts would wrestle him but sometimes some fellow up in the States would hear about him and come down for a match... but he came only once!

Jasper was the champion runner.

We used to have a place where we raced, down on Sand Creek, right on the line between Kansas and the Indian Territory.

We started at the creek and ran to the top of the hill and back. It was three and one-half miles from the start and back again.

We ran about two hundred yards to the creek and jumped it, and then on through the grass to the top of the hill.

When a man reached the top of the hill there was a pile of rocks he had to climb up onto and wave back to the fellows at the starting line. They always knew how many men there were in the race and if any of them failed to wave from the top of the hill he was disqualified.

In that part of the Indian Territory, at that time, there were Cherokee, Osage, Delaware and Quapaw Indians, Whites, Mexicans and Negroes, all vying for supremacy.

Sometimes there were two or three races a week but there was always one on Sunday.

When the Ponca Indians came over there was always a good race and even though Jasper Exendine was the best man, that didn't keep them from trying.

FOOT RACING ON SUNDAY

One Sunday a couple of runners came down from Independence, Kansas. They were good but not at the distance so they challenged Jasper to a three-hundred-yard dash.

I don't see how such a big man carried that much beef as fast as he did, but he won by fifteen feet; and he carried off, in winnings, the other man's pony, three blankets and his watch. It was a bad day for the challenger!

There was a pretty little Osage girl who lived down on Bird Creek. Her name was Rosie Red Eagle; she was a sister of Red Eagle. They were camped up near us and all the boys wanted to marry Rosie.

One Sunday Rosie said she would marry the man who won that day and about seventy-five of the boys got into the race. Three runners came down from Independence to try to win the race and Rosie!

There was a wild scramble and all the boys did their best; but Jasper came in first, and he was already married, so nobody got to marry Rosie!

WILD HAY

My stepfather had a side camp on Fish Creek about twelve miles southwest of the home place.

The land was covered with tall wild hay as far as the eye could see.

In the fall, 1877, he took my brother and me with a bunch of hands and went down there to put up hay for the winter-feeding.

We took with us mowers, rakes and buck rakes, or as they called them, "go-devils."

Dick Mooney, Roddy Green, Jim Hymer and I went as hay pitchers. Luther Green, and old man Higbee were the stackers. Dan Modene, my brother, my stepfather and Jim Hymer were the teamsters. Fred Kraut took his team and went along as utility man, and the cook was Sam Collins.

We arrived at the side camp early and made camp.

Dan Modene cut around a large piece of grassland. The rule was that no one could cut hay inside of a piece of land another man had cut around.

We cleaned out the spring and fixed up the corral and feed racks and rode around the horse pasture, which was only about one hundred acres, and repaired the fence.

The boys turned their ponies into the pasture, hung up their saddles in the trees and tied their slickers over them, took their bedding into the tent and got ready for work.

The next morning Dan and Jean started mowing around a twenty-acre plot. Fred did the raking.

After dinner Charlie Coulson and Henry Wagon started the go-devils.

They would rake the hay in huge loads up to the stacks and the pitchers would pitch it onto the stacks, then the stackers did the rest.

It was hot as love in August and the stackers would come down while the go-devil teams were resting.

They would razz each other and banter to see which crew could put up the most hay in one day.

Then for fear the other team might get the start of them they would both go back to work again.

The machines would go from sunrise to sundown.

The hay that was cured must all be in the stack every night for fear of rain.

Each stack was fenced, plowed around, then a fire guard burned all around. That was so the stacks would be protected in case of fire. Safeguarded in this way the hay would stand there until they were ready to feed it to the stock.

It took about a week to put up all the hay they wanted, but Saturday night they were through, with one hundred seventy-five tons in the stacks and the fireguards all plowed around them.

They all planned to go home on Sunday.

FUN IS WHERE YOU FIND IT

There was a dance that night at Sam Whiteturkey's.

Roddy Green, Jim Hymer, another boy named Bill and I saddled our ponies and started home right after supper.

We were all young and full of life and mischief and hadn't had any fun in a long time. Katie Whiteturkey would be there and we might get to dance with her.

Katie was the belle of the Cherokee Nation.

She was a full-blooded Delaware girl, robust and very pretty. She had been down to the Cherokee Seminary, near Park Hill, not far from Tahlequah, and she spoke good English, much better than the rest of us, Indians or otherwise.

As we rode by John Sarcoxie's place we saw he had some geese shut up in a corncrib so we stopped and took them out. Pulling out some of their feathers, so John could track them easily, we put them across the road in Jim Wind's corncrib.

We rode on laughing and wondering what would happen when John found his geese in Jim's corncrib.

We made our own fun in those days with the material at hand.

Down where the road crossed Hog Shooter Creek there was a large deep pool of water at the bottom of a cliff.

The cliff ran straight up about ten feet. At the top, for about forty feet back the land was as flat as a table. This was a place where hunters camped when they came down from the States to shoot game.

We who lived there never killed the game for sport, so there was no love for the hunters from the States, who wasted the game.

They ran the deer with greyhounds and scared away what they did not kill or cripple and they left the crippled deer to die without trying to track them down.

To us it was a violation of the code of our country.

As we rode up to the creek we saw a party of hunters from the States camped on the flat above.

They had a wagon sheet on their wagon and it was backed up close to the edge of the cliff with rocks back of the wheels to keep the wagon from rolling off into the pool of water.

The horses were tied to the hind wheels and the harnesses were hung on the wagon tongue.

The hunters were all in the wagon sound asleep.

We looked the situation over and decided to mete out a little justice on behalf of the wild game.

We untied the horses and took the rocks from behind the wheels. Then we all got behind the wagon and gave it a good push. It went over the cliff and slid into the water.

The water was halfway up the wagon-bows and the entire wagon was covered.

We waited until we saw the hunters come out of the wagon, swearing and spitting out the water; then we went back to where we had tied our ponies and rode away laughing about the trick we had played on them.

We felt we had evened up the score for some of the crippled deer the hunters had left to die.

Riding on in the direction of Sam Whiteturkey's, there was a tinhorn doctor, who lived at the east bank of the Caney River, where the road crossed at a ford.

As we approached the ford Jim said, "I'll bet five dollars that damned old cuss ain't had a call in three months and won't have for three months more."

"I'll take that bet," said Roddy, and we wondered what he was thinking.

As we rode up to the house Roddy went up to the yard fence and called the doctor, who, at the second hail, came to the door in his nightclothes.

"Is this where Doctor Lebo lives?" asked Roddy.

"It is," answered Doc.

"Are you him?"

"I am. What can I do for you?"

"A man down at Joe Bennett's has his leg broken. He wants you to come and fix it up for him. We are going to tell his folks up on Post Oak Creek. Now hurry!"

As we rode away into the Caney River we heard Doc come down the hill and hit the trail for Joe Bennett's on a high lope.

"There," says Roddy to Jim, "you lose your five spot. Doc has a call and it won't take him long to cover the five miles down to Joe Bennett's — if he keeps that lick up."

Jim paid off and we were all wondering what to do next when we came in sight of where Frank McMullen lived.

Frank had sort of a bad name and there were not many people who liked him.

As we got even with the house Jim rode up to the fence and called him. He came to the door with his Winchester in his hand.

"Say, Frank," called Jim, "the marshals are camped down at Silver Lake. They stopped us this evening and wanted to know where you lived and how to get here. It might not mean anything but we thought it would do no harm to tell you."

He turned and ran back to the house calling over his shoulder, "Thanks, fellows." He grabbed his hat and boots, got his gun and another box of cartridges and headed for the Osage Hills, as fast as he could go, and he didn't come back for two weeks.

After that we rode on home.

It was too late for the dance and besides we thought George Wilson had probably got Katie Whiteturkey by that time and none of us would have a chance with her anyhow.

When we got to the Goodhue place, which was my home, we turned our ponies into the feedlot, climbed up in the haymow and went to sleep.

It was well after noon when my stepfather and the rest of the hands got back from the hay camp and although we wanted very badly to know how the hunters came out we wisely refrained from making inquiries about them.

We knew my stepfather would not approve of what we had done.

After we all had our dinner and the horses were cared for we got Jean aside and he told us the wagon was still in the creek when they crossed. They had put in over an hour helping the hunters to get it out and it took three teams to put it on the road again.

The hunters told them their horses were tied to the hind wheels when something scared them, the horses broke loose but the wagon went over the bank and nearly drowned the whole bunch in the creek.

We told Jean what had happened, so we all had a good laugh and really felt justified when Jean told us the hunters had had some greyhounds with them.

I helped to fill the barn, feed racks and sheds and put up the hay at home. When the work was all done I went up to the Owens ranch and they put me on as a line rider.

RIDING FOR THE OWENS CATTLE COMPANY

The Owens Cattle Company had six cabins built around the range they claimed. The cabins were the cowboys' camp and there was a rider in each one.

It was the cowboys' job to ride out along the line until they met the rider from the other camp, then turn around and ride back the other way, until they met the rider from the camp in the opposite direction.

It was the rider's job to turn back any stock that was trying to cross out and stray away.

If he found where a bunch had crossed the trail he read the signs they had left and making a sign for the other rider he took the trail of the strays.

SIGNS

A large cross in the dirt on the trail meant: Stock has crossed here; look for more signs and tracks. An arrow in the dirt meant: Follow. When weeds were broken: Follow the way they are bent.

When the other rider came to the place, he read the signs and also the signs the first rider had left and either followed or rode the entire line according to the signs.

In this manner all the stock were held in a human fence of riders or were quickly returned if they should stray.

TRACKING

One morning I was riding the southeast line when I came to a trail where about thirty head of ponies had crossed out.

Reading the signs I saw they had been driven by three shod ponies. The signs were fresh where they had crossed the creek; the water in the tracks was still muddy.

Making signs for the other rider to follow me I started on the trail of what I felt sure were horse thieves.

I had gone only a few miles when, riding over a hill, I saw the herd about four hundred yards ahead of me.

The thieves were having trouble with them for they did not want to leave the home range and were hard to drive.

As I came over the hill, one of the thieves started back to meet me, shooting as he came.

He had bad luck.

The other two started back to avenge his death. They had a little better luck for they hit me three times before getting theirs.

About that time the other line rider for the Owens outfit came over the hill.

He looked at my wounds and saw they were not going to be fatal.

He tied me on my horse so I would not fall off and together, with three extra ponies and their empty saddles; we followed the herd back home.

He took me to headquarters and went back to his job of double line riding until I was able to ride again.

There was a family camped at the ranch who were moving to Gainesville, Texas. One of their horses had gone lame and they were camping there until it got well.

The mover's wife was a real woman. She had treated gunshot wounds before and I was turned over to her for treatment.

She washed my wounds and laid me out under a tree where the fresh air would heal them faster than anything else.

None of them were very bad and in about four weeks I was well on the way to recovery.

9 MY FIRST WARRANT

IT was about the year 1878, and by this time I had been legally adopted by Jasper Exendine. Jasper and his wife had seemed so lonely my parents had finally given their consent.

In about five weeks after my fight with the cattle thieves I was able to travel and went home to Jasper's.

It was three months later, I should say, when one day a large man on a good horse rode up and asked if that was where Jasper Exendine lived. I told him it was, and he asked: "Is there a young man here named Frank Eaton?"

"You are talking to him right now. What do you want with me?"

The big man looked me over and said: "There is some mistake. You are only a boy. I am looking for the man Chris Adams commissioned as Deputy United States Marshal."

For answer I took out my badge and commission and handed them to him.

"Well I'll be damned! I thought you were older than you are. Chris said you were young, but a good man, and I came to get you. We are camped on Coon Creek and we need another man. I am a marshal out of Judge Parker's court for the Western District of Arkansas." And he showed me his badge.

I told him I would go, saying, "I am not fully recovered yet but if my side gets to hurting I can quit."

"What ails your side?"

"A doggone horse thief put a chunk of lead in it!"

"What happened to him?"

"Oh, he just quit stealing horses."

"Are you the Owens rider that had the fight with horse thieves?"

"I sure am and ready for another one."

"All right. Get your horse and come over on Coon Creek at Joe Mack's place and you can go on active duty right now."

"Wait until I saddle up and I will ride back with you," I told him.

"All right go ahead," said the marshal and he got off his horse and sat on the fence while I got ready to go.

I saddled my pony, led him out of the lot, tied him to the fence and then went into the house for my Winchester and coat.

Telling Jasper good-by and sticking my rifle in the scabbard I told the marshal to lead the way.

He mounted and we rode away.

ONLY ONE PONY TO SPARE

Jake Bartles had a store at the ford on the river so we stopped there and I got another box of forty-fives for my gun. The marshal bought some tobacco and we rode on to the marshal's camp, which was in the barn lot of my old friend, Joe Mack.

Joe was in the yard as we rode up and he hailed me.

"Hello, Pete!" he said, "I told these fellows you would come if you were able to ride."

94

"I thought you said your name was Frank.

Joe here called you Pete and you answered. How come?" asked the marshal who had brought me. Joe laughed.

"Pistol Pete! That is the name Colonel Copinger gave him," Joe said, "and he can make any of you sit up and take notice when it comes to handling a fighting iron. He is good, believe me."

There were four marshals in the camp and five prisoners.

The officers did not believe all that Joe said about my ability to outshoot the best of them and said so very plainly.

"I'll bet you a good pony he can," bet Joe.

"Good enough, we will take that." And they got ready their pony.

"I'll bet you another pony that you lose." Joe felt sure of winning.

They were about to call him when the head marshal said, "Be careful, boys. Chris Adams told me that the boy packs the fastest and truest guns in the Territory. One pony is all we can spare."

"We won't spare him. The boy can't beat all of us."

"All right, let's get busy and see," said the head marshal.

We shot and I beat them badly.

They were marshals and had been trained to shoot.

I was only a boy, but back of me was that patient training of Mose Beaman, the hours of practice that had stretched into months, then years, with always the ever-present possibility of meeting, not just one at a time, the men who had killed my father.

My guns were a part of me. Already my knowledge of how to handle them had made the difference between life and death on more than one occasion.

This was true of the marshals, too, but they hadn't started when they were eight years old. I had.

Joe took the marshals' pony and put him in his barn.

I DRAW A MURDERER

"Say, Boss," said one of the officers, "that kid would be a good man to go after old Jack Schonwaldt. That old cuss will never give up. He knows Judge Parker will hang him if he ever gets a chance and any man had rather die at the muzzle of a gun than at the end of a rope."

"That's just what I had in mind when I saw him make that draw," said the marshal. "The kid can sure shade him."

Next morning after breakfast the head marshal said to me, "Do you know Jack Schonwaldt?"

"Yes, I do."

"Did you ever have any trouble with him?"

"No. I never said a dozen words to him in my life but I know him and know his reputation."

"All right, here is a warrant charging him with murder. Serve it."

"But why all these questions," I asked. "What is the difference if I have had trouble with him or not?"

"Because Jack is a hard man to handle. If you ever had any trouble with him, then had to kill him while he was resisting arrest, someone might think you were just settling an old grudge."

"Well, I'll be doggoned, I never thought of that."

"Perhaps not," said the marshal, "but we must look at all the angles. We have to protect our men all we can. Now, son, be careful and don't let him get the drop on you. Don't shoot unless you have to, but if you have to kill him, bring in his boots and gun. Then we can return the warrant as served. I think he is up on California Creek near John Swanick's place. We will move tomorrow and you will find us somewhere down at Silver Lake. Now once more, be careful."

He turned and walked up to the house. I stood there looking at my first warrant!

COLLECTING PRISONERS

Now in those days the United States Marshals had a team and wagon with a driver who also acted as a guard for the prisoners they collected.

Each marshal usually had along with him four or five Deputy United States Marshals and a cook.

They had a tent and each man had his own bedroll.

They would start from Fort Smith, Arkansas, with a bunch of warrants. When they had served them and had a wagonload of prisoners they would take them back to Fort Smith.

Each man had his own horse and firearms and when they camped for the night they took turns guarding the men they had arrested.

The bad ones were ironed to prevent their escape.

The marshals made camp at some central point and while the cook and the driver guarded the prisoners the rest of the men would scour the country with their warrants.

The prisoners weren't taken in until a load was collected, which was taken to Fort Smith, where the old Federal Jail was.

There the prisoners were turned over to Judge Isaac C. Parker.

The judge gave them another batch of warrants and they started out again.

They kept this up the year round except when winter weather made it impossible to travel that way. Then the warrants just had to wait until spring.

I left the camp and started out to serve my first warrant. I rode up past the head of Coon Creek and out on the big prairie that reached from the Caney River to the Verdigris River. It was covered with tall grass.

I rode at a trail gait, in the direction of John Swanick's place, across the prairie, and covered the ground at a moderate pace.

There were bunches of cattle and horses grazing in the tall rank grass and occasionally a deer would jump up and run away, then he would stop out of range and look at me as I rode past.

OLD FRIENDS

As I approached the Swanick range I saw more cattle and ponies and at last saw a rider coming toward me. I changed my course and rode to meet him and was overjoyed to find it was my friend and old playmate Jonas Swanick, John Swanick's son. When he recognized me he gave a wild whoop and we rode to meet each other at full speed.

"Frank," he cried, "how do you happen to come? We were talking about you last night. Dad was saying how much he would like to see you."

"Well, here I am and I sure will be glad to see him. Say, pardner, you're looking as fat as an export steer. I'll bet Johnnie Wind can't throw you now."

"No," said Jonas, "I wallowed him good and plenty down at the races last Sunday. We sure had a hard tussle but he had to own up that I was the best man . . .. I've seen to all the cattle, so we can go to the house now. You are going to stay with me awhile and we will go deer hunting again. You won't beat me so bad this time — I'm a lot better shot than I was last time we went hunting!"

We rode up toward the house talking and laughing — just two youngsters happy to see each other.

We turned our ponies loose in the feedlot and walked up to the house.

John Swanick was a full-blooded Delaware Indian a little more than six feet tall. With the exception of Jasper Exendine he was the best wrestler, jumper and foot racer in Cooweescoowee District.

He was sitting out by the side of the house and came to meet me with his hands reached out in greeting. "Hello, my boy, I am glad to see you and find you looking so well. We were just talking about you last night and wondering when you would come. Oh, Jane, here is Frank!"

Mrs. Swanick came in from the kitchen. The Indian women are not very demonstrative but she shook hands with me and patted me on the shoulder. "It's a long time we don't see you, son. How come?"

I told them all the things that had happened since I last saw them and explained that I had been as busy as a one-armed man in a swarm of buffalo gnats and was just getting around again.

"We heard about your fight with the white-man thieves, "she said; "we are sure glad you fight so good. We like to tell everybody you are our friend, but you must be more careful for we won't want you killed."

With a final pat on the shoulder she went back to the kitchen and we all sat around and talked until supper was ready.

At the supper table I asked about Jack Schonwaldt.

99

Mrs. Swanick started and Jonas and his father looked at me intently. "Why do you want to know?" asked John. "He is a dirty, mean Dutchman, no good at all. He is just a fast shooter and a mean man. He has a camp about a mile up the creek, on my land, and he won't get off. There are some more men up there with him who came down from the States. I think they steal the Indians' cattle and hogs and butcher them, then take them up to Sedan and Cherryvale, Kansas, and sell them to the butchers. Sometimes they are gone a long time and come back with lots of paper money. He is no good."

"Is he here now?" I asked.

"Yes, he came in yesterday. That is why we were talking about you. You are a marshal now, maybe you can stop him."

"Well, I am here now and in the morning I will ride up there and try to bring him in."

"We will go help you," said John.

"No, if we were all to ride up there, he would be on the lookout; somebody would get hurt. I think it would be best if Jonas and I ride out and look about the ponies then come back that way past his place. That way, maybe we can get the drop on him and bring him in without any trouble."

"Maybe you are right," said John, "and if you don't get the drop on him you can ride around the bend of the creek and tie your ponies. Then go up through the paw-paws and try to get him that way. But he knows you are a marshal and if he thinks you are after him he is going to kill you on sight."

BOOTS AND GUN

"I have a warrant for him for murder, and I intend to serve it. If he resists arrest one of us will sling hash in hell tomorrow night."

100

The next morning as Jonas and I rode away Mrs. Swanick called out to us to be careful while she stood in the yard and watched us ride out to where the cattle and ponies were feeding.

We were riding through the cattle when Jonas rode up to me and said, "By garr, Frank, here he comes right now."

I knew Jack Schonwaldt was a dangerous man, and I was on my guard. That was a good thing for me for I didn't think he would do the thing he did. But when you know your life is at stake you are going to be ready for anything.

Jack Schonwaldt was riding right toward us.

"Keep about twenty yards out to one side of me," I told Jonas, "so we won't both be in front of him."

Jonas rode over to look at a yearling.

"Hello, Jonas," said Jack as he rode up.

Then he turned to look at me. He recognized me and without a word he made a lightning grab for his gun.

I was ready for him and Jack pitched off his horse, firing two shots that went wild as he fell.

"You fellows never let me do nothin'," complained Jonas, who had drawn too late to shoot.

"You may get action yet," I told him. "There are a couple of fellows coming out from the cabin."

"They are his friends from the States and maybe we will have to kill them, too."

Jonas was ready for battle.

101

"Let's wait and see what they do," I cautioned him; "they may not want to fight."

The strangers rode up and we watched them closely.

"Hello," cried one of them, "what's going on here? Anyhow, who are you?" he asked, addressing me.

"I am Frank Eaton, a Deputy United States Marshal," I said. "I had a warrant for this man but he drew his gun when he recognized me without giving me a chance to arrest him."

Then I looked him in the eye and said, "What is your interest in this game anyhow? Do you want to take a hand?"

"Not by a damn-sight," he said. "I know who you are. But we just came down from Havana and stayed all night with Jack. What are you going to do with him now?"

"Plant him, I guess, after I get his boots and gun to show that the warrant was served."

"We will take him to Havana and bury him if you don't care."

"That's all right. All I want is his boots and gun."

"Here comes Dad," says Jonas. "He has somebody with him and I believe they are in a hurry."

John Swanick and the other man were riding toward us as fast as their ponies could run.

John had his Winchester in his hand and was bareheaded, his long hair streaming in the wind, his fine face and regular features looking like a statue come to life.

COUNTERFEIT MONEY

"We heard the shooting," John said, "and came as fast as we could. This is Ed Saunders, the sheriff of Cooweescoowee District."

We shook hands and the sheriff said, "Have you got these other men under arrest?"

"No, I have a warrant only for Jack."

"Damn the warrant! Put up your hands, fellows. I am the sheriff and I am arresting you for stealing cattle and for making counterfeit money. Disarm them, Frank, and see that they don't throw anything away."

I disarmed them and Ed Saunders and John Swanick searched the men.

The sheriff took a large roll of bills from each of them and put the handcuffs on them. Then he searched Jack Schonwaldt's body and found another roll of bills and some coins. He looked at the money and pronounced it all counterfeit.

Then he said, "Put Jack on his pony, boys, and we will go and search the cabin."

At the cabin we found all kinds of molds and equipment and a shot sack full of counterfeit coins. The sheriff took it all with him.

We buried Jack Schonwaldt near his cabin and then we all went down to Swanick's place. It was still early in the day and after dinner Ed Saunders, Jonas and I rode off with the prisoners.

Ed and Jonas were taking their men down to Dog Creek to put them in jail and I rode with them as far as Silver Lake where the marshals were camped.

The head marshal talked with Ed and Jonas and they told him the story of the killing and arrest. He wanted to take the sheriff's prisoners to the Federal Jail at Fort Smith but Saunders would not give them up.

I took the Schonwaldt warrant from my saddle pocket and gave it to the marshal, then I untied my slicker from the back of my saddle and handed him the boots and gun. He threw them into the back of the wagon.

WE LOSE A MARSHAL

That afternoon the head marshal came into camp in a hurry, calling out, "Get your gun, Pete, and come with me. There is hell to pay up the river. I was after Basil Underwood and his gang and Josh Wilson was helping me. We found them and they whipped us bad. Wilson was killed and they shot my hat all to hell! I came for you for I want to be sure to get them. You are a better shot than any of them."

I was ready and we rode off to take the trail of the killers.

We rode for five days and most of the nights, stopping only to get enough rest to go on.

We slept with our hats on, our hands on our guns and our horses ground-hitched beside us, but we never saw or heard tell of Underwood or his gang.

At last we went back to camp.

There was a load of prisoners by this time and we left in a couple of days for Fort Smith. When we arrived there, we were given a week to rest and get ready for the next trip.

FRED NAIL

It had been a long time since the boys had been in town and they were spending the week trying to have some fun.

In our outfit there was a young Cherokee Indian named Fred Nail who was a Deputy United States Marshal.

He was about six feet and one inch tall, weighed about two hundred ten pounds, was raw-boned with heavy muscles. He had a clear light bronze skin and regular features.

Fred was handsome and a good clean boy.

He got stuck on one of the girls at the Pea Green Dance Hall.

A Fort Smith city policeman named Surratt was also mighty fond of her and one night the two men came together.

Nail had no gun because the marshals were not allowed to carry their guns to the dance halls and saloons, but Surratt, as an officer, had his gun on.

The two men got into a fight and Surratt pulled his gun and Fred Nail took it away from him and knocked him down with his fist.

Surratt got up and left and Nail gave the gun to the man who ran the dance hall.

But Surratt got another gun and came back.

Fred Nail was sitting at a table with his back to the door, when Surratt came in and shot him in the back without warning, killing him instantly.

The police arrested him, of course; he didn't have nerve enough to resist an armed man. They took him away for fear a mob would form and hang him or some of the marshals would shoot him for the brutal cowardly trick.

I was at the camp when the murder took place.

The boys all had to leave their guns at camp when out seeing the town but I always stayed with my gun in those days.

When the news came I was one of the first to reach the scene.

There were four wagons of marshals in town and in half less than no time the town was filled with armed men all ready to avenge their comrade and feverish for action.

There were not enough men in town to stop a mob if one got started but some of the older heads got them quieted down and no one else was killed.

I had never seen a man shot in the back before and the dirty, cowardly murder made a lasting impression on me as it did on all the others.

The head marshals hurriedly outfitted their wagons and left town with their men before there was any more trouble.

THE FIGHT AT COODYS BLUFF

We were after a bunch of outlaws at a place called Coodys Bluff, which was over in the eastern part of the Indian Territory almost to the Arkansas line.

Our camp was on a little creek at the foot of a bluff.

The Bill Pidgeon gang of outlaws was in a cabin on top of the bluff about a half-mile away.

There were four of them and they were wanted for everything from petty larceny to murder.

The land sloped in all directions from the cabin and there were very few trees but lots of big, high grass.

East of the cabin was a gully with high steep banks and at the foot of the bluff was a big spring.

The cabin, probably twelve by fourteen feet, was made of logs and was chinked and daubed. Some of the cracks had the chinking knocked out and the gang was using the cracks for portholes.

In front of the door, a little way out, was a great big snag of a bur-oak tree, with the top broken out of it. The tree was dead and nearly four feet through; it had been big and tall but the men had used the top for wood.

We had the outlaws surrounded and had been exchanging shots with them all day but no one was hurt that we knew of.

The head marshal was a man by the name of J. A. Wilkinson; he was out with us.

I was on the first watch with Wilkinson, from dark until eleven o'clock. Then we slept until about an hour before daylight.

Wilkinson said, "Let's slip up and hide behind that big tree and see if we can't get a shot at them in the morning that will do some good." The tree was big enough so we could both hide behind it.

Just as it was coming daylight Wilkinson said to me, "Wonder if they're still in there? You look around your side of the tree and I will look around mine."

I took my hat off and looked very carefully while Wilkinson looked around the other side.

Our boys in the hollow were watching us.

Just about the time I got my head around so I could see even with the door in the cabin, a piece of bark hit me in the face and a bullet went into the stump of the tree.

I said, "Yes, by gad, they're in there!"

Wilkinson laughed. He was a big fleshy man and when he laughed he shook all over.

Every time we showed any part of our clothing they put a bullet in it. They were good marksmen, but they didn't dare come out of the house to rush us for they would be under the fire of our boys.

It was fun for a while.

We would stick a rag around the tree and the outlaws would shoot at it. Then our boys would fire at the smoke from their guns.

But it was summer and there was no shade, and pretty soon that smoke began to make us drier than a powder horn. Neither of us had taken any water with us and I got so dry I could hardly stand it.

About ten or eleven o'clock I said, "I am going to get a drink of water."

Wilkinson said, "Yes, and they will slap a chunk of lead through you."

But I thought I had just as soon be shot as starve for water.

I stuck my gun in the holster good and tight and pulled the buckenstring over it and took my rifle in one hand and my hat in the other. I jumped about six feet right straight out from that tree and then started running jig-jag for the hollow.

The outlaws fired a few shots when I first jumped out; then they just laughed. One of them hollered, "Run, you son of a gun!" but I couldn't run any faster.

I made it down where our boys were in nothing flat and the whole bunch was laughing.

I just sat there a minute and got my wind, then went on down to the gully and on down to the spring. I got a drink of water and sat back to rest behind a real thick cedar bush. Thought I would rest a minute and take another drink. There wasn't a breath of air stirring and it sure was hot.

I sat back and looked up at the cabin. It was about sixty yards from the spring to the top of the bluff and the cabin set back about ten feet from the edge of the bank.

Pretty soon I saw a trail all covered over with brush, green briars and blackberry bushes until I could hardly see the ground. A man could walk down that trail from the house to the spring and he couldn't be seen with a spyglass, if he was careful and walked stooped over.

I thought I saw a twig move, up near the top, but decided it must be a bird — when directly, about ten or fifteen feet farther down the trail, I saw another bush move.

I just sat right quiet behind that rifle with my gun cocked and the muzzle stuck through the cedar bush so I could cover the trail and the spring, too, and waited.

Before long one of the outlaws, a man named Dick Van, came out of the brush. He had a rifle in one hand and a wooden bucket in the other. He stood still and looked all around. I waited because I had him covered. He set the rifle down and dipped his bucket into the spring.

I said, "Don't straighten up, Dick, just stay as you are, drop your gun and unbuckle your belt." He couldn't see me and didn't know where I was but I was to the side of him not over ten feet away.

He unbuckled his belt and dropped his gun. I said, "Now back away from there with your hands up."

He said, "I'm going to get a drink of water even if you shoot me," and I knew just how he felt.

"All right, dip your bucket and back off and take a drink." He did.

I told him to fill the bucket and start down to our camp. When we got there I sat him down on the ground in front of the wagon, stuck his feet through the spokes in a front wheel and put the shackles on his legs.

Then I put his hands above the hub and put the handcuffs on him. Dick was a bad man and I was not taking any chances with him.

I turned around and got a biscuit and apiece of meat and another drink of water and started back.

As I passed the wagon Dick threw the handcuffs to me and said, "Unlock these things." His hands were smaller than his wrists and we couldn't keep a handcuff on him so I took my cuffs and told the guard to watch him pretty close and I went back to the spring.

I crawled up the trail to see how Wilkinson was making it and I saw how they had the trail fixed.

The trail led to the top of the bluff and just under the edge they had a tunnel to the house with a trap door in the floor.

I knew they must be getting pretty dry so after telling the boys what I was going to do I just stayed by that tunnel. Wilkinson stayed behind the tree until dark then made his getaway without drawing a single shot.

A little after dark we took a stick of dynamite, lit the fuse and threw it in the tunnel. We blew that old cabin all to pieces.

We got two of the men and they were not hurt but Bill Pidgeon, the leader, got away.

We went back to our camp and waited until morning.

As soon as it was light enough Wilkinson and I took his trail. We tracked him for almost seventy-five miles and found where he had got a fresh pony and gone on.

Our horses were dead tired and we tried to get fresh mounts but no one would give us any help at all. Anyone would help Bill Pidgeon, but the marshals could not expect help in those days.

We rested awhile and were riding on slowly down near Vian when we saw two horses tied together down the road and two boys with hunting rifles looking down at two dead men in the road. The boys were waiting for us to ride up.

When we got there we found one of the dead men was Bill Pidgeon and the other Jack Doubletooth, a noted gunman and Bill's deadly enemy.

Both men were full-blooded Cherokee Indians and both had fought in the battle of Pea Ridge in the War between the States.

Bill Pidgeon was in the Confederate Army and Doubletooth in the Union. They had been enemies ever since that battle and had never had a chance to settle it until that day.

The boys told us they had been out hunting and had seen the two men meet. They thought there was going to be a fight so went up to see. The men were talking when the boys got there.

The men got off their horses, tied the bridle reins together and led their horses off the trail where they would not get hurt. Then they stepped up in the trail and turned their backs together, back touching back.

They walked away from each other, ten short steps, counting them aloud so the other could hear. They turned around and started toward each other, firing as they came. When they came together both had emptied their guns.

Both were badly wounded but they fell on their knees and drew their bowie knives and stabbed and cut at each other until they were both dead.

Both men were cut to ribbons, Pidgeon had five bullet holes through him and Jack Doubletooth had four.

They were too good fighters to let the wolves get, so we buried them with their guns and knives on them.

The two boy hunters took the ponies and Wilkinson and I went back to camp.

We had found our man but we didn't take his boots and gun for we hadn't killed him and were not entitled to take them in. They belonged to Jack Doubletooth — but he didn't have any use for them now. Taking the boots and gun of a man you didn't kill was just like an Indian's taking

the scalp of a man he didn't kill. That would bring him nothing but bad luck and he was liable to lose it and his own, too, at the same time.

10 BUD WELLS

TWO MEN

OUR outfit of marshals was camped on a stream tributary to the Illinois River when the boss came in one day and said, "Say, Pete, I am going to let you go down to look for Henry Hinkel, a whisky peddler, who has sold enough whisky to the Indians to put the Arkansas River out of banks. He is the hardest man to catch we ever got after. He has never been arrested, although we have been after him for over a year, and we all have orders to take him any time we can find him. He left Fort Smith with a load of whisky and I think you will find him somewhere in or around Webbers Falls. He is not a gunman but the hardest man to catch I ever saw. He sure will give you action."

"Oh yes . . ." the head marshal continued . . . "look at this picture. Look good, for this is Bud Wells, and he is wanted for murder. He has killed three officers, one of them a Texas Ranger, and you know what that means. Don't take any chances at all with him, for he is paid for and there would be nothing but rejoicing at his funeral."

I looked at the picture and read the description on the back.

Then I looked at the picture again; I wanted it to be photographed on my memory. After studying it a little longer I handed it back to him. "I will start in the morning," I said and went to put another box of ammunition in my saddle pockets.

I also put in some horseshoe nails, a hammer and some pincers, in order to be able to fasten on a shoe if my horse lost one or if one got loose.

As the sun came up the next morning I started out. I went as far as Bill Downing's that day and stayed all night there. Bill told me the most likely place to find Hinkel would be at Ellis Collins's place southwest of Webbers Falls.

He said Hinkel always went there and they would hide him to throw the officers off the trail. "They will lie and tell you he has not been there while at the same time he is out in the haymow, sleeping. You must be careful of such people. Don't trust them."

The next day I was on my way again.

When I crossed the river, it was so low my pony did not need to swim.

About midday I rode into Webbers Falls, a place that had only two stores and very few houses.

There were a few loafers around the stores and I sat around awhile, but it seemed as if they wanted me to leave. Finally I did, riding out southwest on a cow trail.

I saw a man mount his pony and ride out in the same direction. Hiding in the brush I let him go by, then followed him, keeping out of sight all I could.

After a while the man turned in toward a house beside the trail and I saw him talking to a man who had come out in the yard to meet him.

THE WHISKY PEDDLER

I rode up and asked them the directions to the Reed and Palone settlement. They told me, and while I was getting a drink and watering my pony I heard the rider call the other man Ellis. So I knew I had found Ellis Collins, and from their actions I knew Hinkel, the whisky peddler, was around someplace.

Riding out on the trail toward Reed and Palone's I turned off and making a detour came back up behind the Collins barn just in time to see Hinkel riding into the timber half a mile away.

114

The chase was on. Hinkel had a good horse and was riding him for everything there was in him. I knew it was going to be a long ride or a quick fight and sent my pony at top speed.

After a while Hinkel turned off the trail and ran for the timber bottoms.

I followed almost within gunshot but he knew the timber and turned sharply and got out of sight.

I followed the trail like a hound and before long spied my man again.

I fired a couple of shots in hopes of hitting his horse but was too far away. Waving his hat at me he hit the tall timber again and disappeared.

I trailed him until it got too dark to follow, then got off my pony and led him, following my man at a fast walk.

In about three hours I saw a campfire. I tied my pony and went forward to investigate.

It was an hour before I found a trick had been played on me: Hinkel had started the fire, had put on wood and then ridden on, knowing I would spend some time looking for him: no one would ride up to the campfire of the man he was chasing without first looking around for an ambush.

I spent the rest of the night at the campfire and took the trail in the morning.

After following it for about five miles I found where Hinkel had stayed until daylight. His trail was fresh and in the middle of the afternoon I saw my man again. He was about a mile ahead and when he saw me he started running. I gave chase but had no luck and Hinkel took refuge in the brush.

It went on that way for two days and our ponies had almost given out when on the evening of the third day I found Hinkel's horse and learned from a settler that Hinkel had traded him for a fresh horse about two hours before.

But the man had no more horses to trade and I went on with my tired mount.

I followed the trail to the Red River and found that Hinkel had crossed that morning heading for Gainesville, Texas.

By this time my grub was all gone and I rode on to Dexter and laid in a supply.

I went on to Gainesville and found that my man had not been there and I could find no trace of him.

Finally I turned for camp. About three hundred miles away, at Tishomingo, I had my horse shod and went on to Webbers Falls.

BUD WELLS

As I rode up to Si Ringo's store in Webbers Falls, I saw a horse tied to the hitch rack. He was a beautiful animal, a blaze-faced sorrel, with a light mane and tail. He was perfectly proportioned and shod all around. There was a good Texas saddle on him and a thirty-thirty in the scabbard. It was a strange outfit and I looked at it closely while tying my horse.

As I entered the store I saw a man sitting at the far end of the counter, eating. There was something familiar about him. He was about six feet tall and would weigh around one hundred and seventy. He was a fine-looking man, light-complexioned with blue eyes, sandy hair and regular features. He had an honest face. He didn't look like a killer but he was one.

He was dressed in blue jeans, a blue-and-white-striped hickory shirt, shop-made boots and big buckskin Mexican hat with a rattlesnake band.

I could not remember where I had seen him but my sixth sense warned me he was an enemy.

Asking for some canned wieners and some crackers I sat down on a stool at the other end of the counter, facing the stranger, who watched me closely but kept on eating. We ate in silence for a few minutes and then the stranger said:

"Pardon me, boy, are you Frank Eaton?"

"I sure am!"

"Do you happen to have a warrant for me?"

"I don't know. I have several warrants. One of them may be yours. What is your name?"

"My name is Bud Wells! If you have a warrant for me don't try to serve it. I would hate to shoot a boy."

"I don't have a warrant for you but I do have orders to bring you in and I am sure going to do it."

"Like hell you will! Better men than you have tried it and they are pushing up the grass roots now! But let's finish our dinner before we start anything. I would hate to send you to hell on an empty stomach."

"The same back at you," I said, "and we can wait till after dinner to start."

"Say, pardner," said Bud, "let's have the winner pay for both feeds; I have enough money."

"I have enough," I agreed. "Si can collect from the boss if I don't have."

"Si won't be here," said that individual, reaching for his hat. "If you damn fools want to smoke things up I am going for a walk." Putting on his hat he stood by the back door and watched us.

We both laughed heartily and Si grinned but countered: "Laugh, you damn fools, but remember he who laughs last, laughs the longest," and he stood a little closer to the door.

Bud finished eating first and stood by the counter rolling a smoke.

IF MY TIME HAD COME . . .

I wiped the grease off my thumb and thought what a fine thing it would be if I could shoot Bud's gun out of his hand and take him in alive.

I had begun to feel that as a marshal I was just sort of a hired killer and I was tired of it.

Besides I had never taken in a prisoner and he would be a good one to start on. I made up my mind to try it.

Bud lit his smoke and looked at me and Si struck out of the back door on the run. We both laughed and Bud said, "Well, kid, are you ready?"

I had been watching him roll his smoke and his fingers were perfectly steady. All the time he must have been thinking that either he or I would be dead in a few minutes. I got up and stood facing him.

"Yes, I'm ready. Get your iron!"

We both drew.

Bud's gun went off just a split second late and fell on the floor.

My bullet had hit the handle of his gun and grazed across the palm of his hand making an ugly wound.

I kicked his gun out of reach, covered him, and said, "Don't try for it, Bud, or I'll burn you down!"

Stooping over Bud picked up his smoke with his left hand and puffed on it a few times, to see if it had gone out, then he looked me in the eye.

118

"You win, kid," he said, "You beat me. I didn't think the man lived who could do it. Where in hell did you learn how to shoot? How did you make that draw? I'll bet you are a Texan!"

"Wrong! I learned them both in Kansas."

"Like hell you did! No damn Jayhawker ever did draw and shoot likes that. But why didn't you drill me?"

"You are too good a man to kill. I wanted to give you a chance to live a good clean life."

"Damned small chance I'll have if old Parker gets hold of me," said Bud.

"He hasn't got you yet," I told him. "Now I wonder if there is a doctor here to tie up that hand of yours."

HE GAVE HIS WORD

"Tie it up yourself.

Say, Pete, if you won't put the irons on me I will give you my word that I will not try to get away till after you turn me over to your boss."

"Fair enough," I said, "and I will give you a good word to the boss." I tied up his hand.

We went out the door together and I picked up Bud's gun as we went. Si was coming back to the store and I paid for our dinners and we mounted and rode for the Childers Ferry.

"Why don't you take this rifle?" asked Bud, pointing to the thirty-thirty I had seen in the scabbard.

"I have one and also your word and that is all I want."

"Kid, you are a man," said Bud. "I will be as good as my word. If I get out of this, I give you my word, I will stay out of trouble from now on."

119

"Good. If you ever need any help let me know."

We stayed all night at Jim Childers's and Mrs. Childers dressed Bud's hand and gave him some medicine to put on it when it got to hurting too bad.

In the morning Jim put us across on the ferry and wished us luck and we rode on.

The next four days we rode together looking for the marshal's camp. At night we camped and slept on the ground with the loaded rifle still in the scabbard on Bud's saddle.

He had given his word and he stayed with it.

We rode into camp late in the afternoon and the boss and the boys were all there. They came up as we dismounted. I told them of my trip and how Hinkel outwitted and outran me, they all laughed.

"How come you brought this man in?" asked the boss.

Just because he was a better man than I was," said Bud. "He beat me fair and square."

I told my story.

"You shot at his hand and not at his heart?" asked the boss.

"Yes, I did!"

"Well if you are not one of the Lord's own chosen damn fools then I never saw one. That kind of luck won't last always. I don't want you bringing any more prisoners in with a loaded thirty-thirty on their saddle. Now mind that!" and he gave orders for the boys to put the irons on Bud.

After they dressed his hand they let him go with the other prisoners under the guard of one deputy and the driver.

U.S. Marshals At Fort Smith, Arkansas

DEPUTIES HAD HABITS TOO

The next day after my pony had rested I asked the boss if I could go back down to the Ellis Collins neighborhood and see if Hinkel, the whisky peddler, had showed up yet.

"Sure. Give him hell! We've tried to get him for a long time and he's always slipped out some way; while your luck is good, crowd it."

The next morning I started out again after the slippery whisky peddler.

When I got to the Childers Ferry there was a Deputy United States Marshal there from one of the other outfits.

His name was Baz Reed; he was a Creek Indian and I had met him at Fort Smith.

Baz was a small man but a good shot and a good officer.

He was on his way to collect old man Hapgood for selling whisky to the Indians, so we rode on together.

We rode for days and covered a lot of territory. Baz finally got his man, but in all our riding we heard nothing of Hinkel.

One night after we made camp I rode off to scout the Ellis Collins place to see if I could find any trace of him. I promised Baz to be back by daylight if I did not find him.

Baz put the irons on old man Hapgood and after supper he staked out the ponies and bedded down beside his prisoner.

Now Baz had a fool habit of taking off his pants, folding them on top of his boots and putting them under his head for a pillow, and he did it that time.

They had ridden hard all day and he was soon sound asleep.

I came in a little before daylight and the camp was very still. Baz was sound asleep but the old man was gone.

"Hey there, Baz," I hollered, "Where's your prisoner?"

Baz sat up and looked at the old man's empty blanket. He grabbed for his boots and pants, only

to find that his pants were gone and the handcuffs and shackles were lying by his saddle.

Hapgood had taken the keys out of the pants pockets, unlocked the irons, saddled his pony and ridden off, taking the pants with him.

I laughed at my companion's plight, suggesting he cut a three-cornered piece from his saddle blanket, saying that would be specially suitable for a man who slept that sound.

"You go to hell!" said Baz and he made a fire and roasted some meat for breakfast.

After breakfast we started for the store.

"Now, Pete," said Baz, "when we get near the store, I will wait. You go in and get me a pair of pants."

"All right, give me the money and I will buy you a whole suit."

"Money hell! All my money was in my pants and that old cuss is counting it right now. But just wait! I'll see him again!"

We rode on and the horseflies and the mosquitoes kept Baz busy along with telling what he was going to do to old man Hapgood.

When we got about a quarter of a mile from the store Baz stopped and said, "Now, Pete, you go in and buy me some pants and I will wait here."

"All right, Baz. Shall I send them out to you by one of the girls down at the store?"

"It would be just like you to do that very thing. Now hurry up. I want protection from these damned flies."

I rode down to the store and told Si Ringo of the fix that Baz was in.

So we fixed up a reception for him. We looked all through a pile of bib overalls that Si had got in for the cotton pickers. At last we found a pair that would fit a man six feet tall and almost that broad.

Si did them up and I took them out to where Baz was waiting. Baz unwrapped them, looked at them and then at me, started to swear but changed his mind. With a broad grin he put them on and began to roll up the legs, which were about eighteen inches too long.

"What was the use getting suspenders?" he said.

123

"I can button them over the top of my head and save wearing a hat. You always were an extravagant cuss that didn't care for expenses."

Baz got on his pony and we rode on to the store.

There was a bunch of men, women and children out in front of the store and someone called out to the ones inside: "Come and look, folks, here comes Daddy Hubbard. You have heard of Mother Hubbard; now come out and see a Daddy Hubbard."

They all came out and stood around and made remarks. Baz looked at me but I was looking solemn as an owl while I busied myself tying my horse.

Then I said, "Come on, Baz, let's go in and eat something."

Baz was the center of attraction and when we were ready to leave we went out the side door.

Just then, riding up was old man Hapgood's son-in-law bringing Baz's pants and all his belongings with a note from the old man.

It was a gloating note about forgetting to leave the pants in the haste of his departure and just added insult to insult.

Baz went out to the barn to change and when he came back told the young man, "Tell your father-in-law I am much obliged for the pants and will ride out and express my thanks in person."

"You will have to ride fast, mister, for he left this morning before sunup with two mighty good ponies. He said he would write us from Gainesville, Texas, when to expect him back with another load of whisky for the Indians."

Everybody laughed — but to Baz, it wasn't funny.

We rode away heading for the ferry and camped that night at the Childers place.

After we spread out our blankets and bedded down for the night Baz lay there thinking. "Say, Pete, do you think that fellow was telling the truth when he said Hapgood had gone to Gainesville?"

"I don't know. He might, but he might not, too. I'll tell you what we can do. You want him and I want Hinkel. Let's cross the river in the morning and ride up the other side and camp; we better swim the river before daylight for they might be watching the ferry. We will stay until about the time for them to be coming back. If they show up we will snag them and take them in."

"Good," says Baz, "we will do that and hope we get them both."

Pulling off his boots and pants and putting them under his head for a pillow he was soon sound asleep.

We swam the river in the morning while it was still dark and rode out of sight of the ferry before we staked our ponies.

Then we took our rifles and went back to where we could watch the ferry and see who made the crossing.

We lay down in the brush and stayed there until noon, and then we fed and watered our ponies and went back again and watched until evening.

After dark we swam the river again and headed for the Ellis Collins place, headquarters for the whisky peddlers. We kept out of sight, scouted the country and watched for two days and nights, then gave it up and headed for the marshals' camp.

When we got there two startling pieces of news awaited us.

Bud Wells had escaped and Captain Sam Sixkiller had just been murdered.

All the marshals were out with the Lighthorsemen after the two men who had killed Captain Sixkiller.

He had been ambushed in the timber while riding alone and the tracks showed the killers had turned and run without going to the body.

Bill Downing had been riding to catch up with the captain and had heard the shots.

Sam had been murdered in cold blood, without warning, before he could even pull his gun.

That was about the year 1879 and upholding the law was a dangerous business in those days.

The posse got the men who killed Captain Sam Six-killer just three miles from the ambush. One was a white man, Al Cunningham, the other a half-breed Negro and Creek Indian, Dick Van, father of the Dick Van I captured at Coodys Bluff.

The two murderers were shot in a fight with the posse, like the dogs they were, and the posse didn't lose a single man in the fight.

HIS WORD WAS GOOD

Years later I received a letter from a merchant in a small town in Texas, but he didn't sign his name Bud Wells!

He said he had quit the owl-hoot trail just as he told me he would and was a respected businessman with a nice wife and family.

I always knew Bud Wells would keep his word.

11 THE BIG DRIVE

THE marshals' wagon went to Fort Smith soon after that.

I rode for a while with several other deputies, to keep down stock thieves, whisky peddlers, and many other kinds of criminals, of which there were plenty in those days.

But the wages were not enough to feed a pony, to say nothing of a man and a horse, so I took a job riding, as a troubleshooter, for the Cattlemen's Association.

The job paid four hundred dollars a year in four payments, one hundred dollars every three months.

We were allowed to work for any of the cattlemen belonging to the association who wanted us, and we had to drop everything and go when they called.

When we were working on a case, they paid our expenses; at other times we paid our own.

DOWN TO TEXAS

Early in the year 1881 Osage Brown and Reed and

Hampton had a government contract to deliver forty-nine hundred head of cattle from north central Texas to the Osage Agency, for the Indians.

The agency was on Bird Creek at the foot of a big bluff.

It consisted of the Indian agency buildings, three or four stores, the livery stable, a hotel, a few dwellings and the Quaker school, on top of the bluff.

The Agency was where the town of Pawhuska, Oklahoma, now stands. The name Pawhuska, in the Osage language, means, "white hair."

When it was just a camp it was named Pawhuska for an Osage Indian chief called White Hair.

Osage Brown took a bunch of cowboys down into Texas to gather up the cattle and I went along as one of the hands.

There were Brown's two sons Alf and Charlie, Dennie Garrett, Joe Pettit, Bob and Dempsey Gilstrap, Bill Keeler, and Sam Collins, the cook.

We took the chuck wagon and some extra ponies and went down southeast of Fort Worth, Texas.

It was early in the spring, the weather was beautiful and there was plenty of grass and water.

Starting from the Osage Agency, we went down by

Bill Rogers's store on Bird Creek.

We crossed the creek and took the same trail I rode to find Shannon Campsey— down to Burke Norton's store on the Arkansas River —then on down the river to Jim Childers's ferry, where we put the wagon across.

Jim Childers and his wife were glad to see me again and I stayed at their house that night and we talked over old times most of the night.

From there the trail went down by Okmulgee, Stonewall and Tishomingo. We crossed Big Red (Red River) at the big bend north of the town of

Gainesville, Texas, then swung west to buy cattle from the ranches.

By the time we got back to the Trinity River we had all our cattle contracted and they were delivered to a point just across the Trinity about four miles east of Forth Worth.

We held the cattle there until the herd was all collected, then we started the drive back to the Indian Territory.

THE DRIVE

We crossed the Trinity River the first day and cut through the cross timbers. There was no trail and the country was rough and brushy, until we hit the old Chisholm Trail below the Red River.

We crossed Big Red at Red River Station. We crossed in the evening so the sun wouldn't shine in the cattle's eyes.

On the south side of the river, where we went in, was a sand bar; so there were hardly any banks at all.

The Red River was down and the cattle had to swim only about fifty feet or so; by angling down the river we had low banks to climb as we came out.

As we were crossing two Indian boys rode up. They were top hands who knew their business and also the river and were a lot of help to us. They rode with us to the Washita River where their folks lived. Osage Brown gave them ten dollars, which was a lot of money in those days, but they were worth every cent of it.

After crossing Big Red we followed the Chisholm Trail for about twenty miles.

The trail was named for Jesse Chisholm who drove the first cattle over it in 1865.

It was the trail over which Texas cattle were driven to Northern markets.

It started at San Antonio, Texas, and went through to Abilene, Kansas.

We left the Chisholm Trail and traveled northeast through some of the finest rangeland in the world. The game was plentiful and coyotes serenaded us every night.

We had plenty of venison to eat and we shot large numbers of snakes just to keep in practice. God, how I hate snakes!

After we left the trail we took things easy for we were in no hurry and the cattle were gaining weight every day.

We had taken only the range run of cattle and some of those poor old cows were pretty thin and slow.

It was sure hard on the drag drivers trying to look after the slow ones.

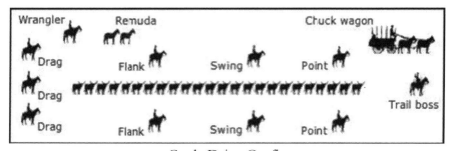

Cattle Drive Outfit

We crossed the Washita River at a riffle. The river was down and it was shallow, but the water was as clear as crystal, so we just watered the cattle and drove them on.

The Canadian we crossed without any trouble even though it is the most treacherous stream in the world. It is worse than the North Canadian and both are full of quicksand; in spots they have no bottom.

After we crossed the Canadian we took it easy until we got to the North Canadian.

The North Canadian was running full and the bank was soft on the north side where we came out.

We went in on the south side and the cattle spread out about a hundred yards in the water and the stronger ones swam upstream against the current but the weaker cattle and the calves were drifted downstream.

QUICKSAND

About thirty feet from the bank I saw Dennie Garrett's horse lunging in the quicksand. The water was about two feet deep and Dennie, who was a long-legged cuss, slid off his horse and tried to help him. But the horse was stuck fast.

One of the boys threw Dennie a lariat and he tied it to the saddle horn and they tried to pull him out that way but he couldn't budge.

I was behind Dennie and I swung in to the cattle to miss the sand hole.

I came near bogging down myself but I made it all right.

While Dennie held the horse's head out of the water and two of the boys pulled on him, I got in and worked his feet out of the sand.

Have you ever heard a horse scream?

It was pitiful to hear the poor thing scream when he found he was fast in the sand. He knew we were trying to get him out and he would turn his head from one to the other begging us not to leave him.

We finally got him out and he was the most grateful critter you ever saw when he felt solid ground under his feet again.

There are many ways of expressing gratitude without saying a word. That horse was talking with his eyes — he was shaking himself and nuzzling all the boys.

Some of the cattle had bogged down in the quicksand on the soft bank, while we were getting him out, so we took off our clothes and went to pulling them out.

131

We worked their tails out first and tied them up over their backs, then worked out a front leg and a hind leg on one side and tied them up. Then we rolled them over and worked out the other two legs and tied them to their bodies.

After we had them tied up we fastened a couple of ropes to their horns and one to their tail and pulled them out on the bank. Then one of us sat on their head while another untied them.

When one of the cows was free we all ran for our horses and mounted as fast as we could for she was not like Dennie's pony; she got up on the prod.

It was a sight to see five or six naked men running like hell to get on their ponies before an old cow could catch them and after driving her off going back in after another one; and it would have to be done all over again.

There were about fifty of the cattle that had to be pulled out but we didn't lose any of them.

When we got them all out we drove them far enough away from the river so that they wouldn't get into the quicksand again.

It was after sundown before we got the wagon across the river and camped for the night.

THE ARKANSAS RIVER

The next morning we headed for the Sac and Fox Agency. It was not far from where Shawnee, Oklahoma, is now.

We swam the Arkansas River all right but it was always deep and swift. We had to float the wagon across on cottonwood logs.

The logs were placed under the wagon bed and the wagon tied down around the coupling poles so it wouldn't come loose and float on down the river.

All the men we could spare got in front of the wagon and towed it across the river.

While we were working on the wagon the team swam across and were waiting at the bank ready to pull it up.

After that the streams were small; and where we had to swim the cattle, it was easy.

THE MEETING PLACE

We were to meet Reed and Hampton at Jesse Creek. Billy Sunday was to be there, too, with one thousand head of cattle from Bearde and Yokum up near Bartlesville.

The last day on the trail we started early and the wind started blowing about the time we got the herd moving.

For three miles we faced the wind and sand. We had bur handkerchiefs over our faces and our hats pulled down. The sand cut like a knife and the air was full of electricity.

When we cracked the whip or the lariat, lightning shot out from the end. The horses ducked their heads and walked sideways.

As we came near Jesse Creek there was a long narrow valley about two miles wide. It was between two hills with rocky slopes and timber-covered tops. They called it Nigger Gap.

We went through the gap in the morning.

The country was covered with waist-high grass and the valley was beautiful.

133

We crossed Jesse Creek as we came out of the gap and the pointers turned the cattle into a natural corral of thousands of acres of land covered with high grass.

Jesse Creek had a rock bottom that was a series of shelves, one just a little higher than the other all along the bank.

It was a beautiful stream. There was a riffle where we crossed and the water was clear as glass. There were holes as much as four feet deep that were filled with fish; big buffalo, catfish and many other kinds, some weighing two or three pounds.

The cattle waded in and drank but paid no attention to the fish.

Jesse Creek ran into Sand Creek and formed a barrier on two sides of the big valley.

On the other two sides a big bluff arose from the edge of the creek. There was a sharp rise covered with grass and brush, then the sandstone rocks of the bluff going straight up; the top was thick with timber.

It was possible to hold an unlimited number of cattle in this natural corral with a small number of men.

About the time we got there we heard Reed and Hampton coming in. They had crossed the Caney River below the mouth of Sand Creek and had come in by Jesse Thompson's place, crossing Jesse Creek right at his house.

In about an hour Billy Sunday's outfit was crossing Sand Creek and coming out on the flat valley.

Osage Brown and his son Alf were counting the cattle as they came through the gap. One stood on each side and we drove the cattle between them.

For every ten cattle they dropped a match in a hat and then they counted the matches.

There were a few over eleven hundred head in Billy Sunday's bunch and that brought the herd up to almost five thousand.

It was almost sundown when we got the cattle all counted in and the first guard on the night herd had gone back to the herd.

JUDGE ISAAC C. PARKER, THE HANGING JUDGE

ALBUQUERQUE, NEW MEXICO, 1880

Pat Garrett, famous sheriff who killed
Billy the Kid, 1881

Blue Duck and his faithful friend,
Belle Starr

138

A GROUP OF UNITED STATES MARSHALS AT FORT SMITH,
ARKANSAS

MY LIFELONG FRIEND ROLLA GOODNIGHT AND ME
ABOUT 1886

ME AND FRIEND WITH ONE OF COLONEL CHARLES
GOODNIGHT'S ORIGINAL CHUCK WAGONS, 1948

COLONEL CHARLES GOODNIGHT

THE OLD FEDERAL JAIL AT FORT SMITH, ARKANSAS

ED WEBSTER AND ME AT THE HEADQUARTERS OF
WEBSTER'S RANCH ON SANO CREEK IN THE CHEROKEE
NATION ABOUT 1887

GARRISON AVENUE, FORT SMITH'S MAIN STREET ABOUT
1872

ALBUQUERQUE JUST BEFORE THE TURN OF THE CENTURY

The wind had quit blowing and a storm was coming up.

While we were eating supper at the chuck wagon the boss came up and doubled the men on the first watch.

Then he called out, "All you other men saddle your best night horse and tie him at your head. We're going to have hell before daylight."

THE STORM

The clouds were banked heavy in the southwest and all the sky was overcast.

It was hot and sultry, not a breath of air stirring; some of the old cows were panting with their tongues sticking out.

The air was charged with electricity, our flesh tingled, and the closer the clouds came the worse it hit us.

As the clouds came closer the lightning came straight down to the ground and the thunder right with it: not a second between the lightning flash and the terrific thunderclap.

Some of the old cows were moaning and making sounds as though they were talking to their calves.

The boys started circle-driving and singing the old Texas Lullaby. You can't hold a herd at night without singing to them, for singing helps to quiet a herd; they know where you are and will stand still as long as they can hear you.

By this time all the boys were out, singing at the tops of their voices.

It started to rain and soon the noise of the storm was so great that the cattle could no longer hear us singing.

The lightning just seemed to play over their backs and little balls of fire were dancing on the ends of their horns.

143

The balls of fire were playing on the ends of the horses' ears, too.

I rubbed my hands down my horse's shoulder and every hair crackled and fire flew in all directions.

All at once there was a big blinding flash of lightning straight down into the ground on a little knoll in the middle of a clump of jack oaks.

I was about four hundred yards in front of where the lightning struck and I knew Bob Gilstrap was behind me someplace.

You couldn't see your hand in front of you and the noise was deafening. My pony stumbled but he got up on his feet again, shook his head and loped on.

I said a scared prayer and started singing an old song about a stampede "gittin' men to pray."

The rain came down in sheets running a foot deep on level ground.

The boys were still circle riding and riding in to break up the mill when an old cow bawled for her calf. The calf answered, and then every cow in the herd went to bawling for her calf and the calves all went to bawling back.

By the lightning flashes I could see an old cow here and there running to one calf and then another smelling for her own. When they found each other the cow stood still and let the calf suck or walked on slowly with the calf at her side.

About three o'clock in the morning the storm began to let up and a little later it started to get light.

We had held the herd!

DAYLIGHT

By the morning light we saw that one of the jack oaks was uprooted and torn all to pieces.

We counted nine dead steers scattered around the knoll, and right in the middle of them Bob Gilstrap was sitting on his horse, with his head bowed down and his hands on his saddle horn, just as though he were asleep.

Some of the boys called to him but he didn't answer.

We went out to lead his pony in. We found that Bob's hair was singed right close to the scalp.

His head was bare. He was alive, but unconscious. His horse had a big singed place across his withers and down his front leg and could hardly walk, but we led him down to the chuck wagon and laid Bob in it.

That morning we started for the Osage Agency with the cattle.

ANOTHER DAY

We had a hard time getting the cattle started.

The herd was so big that it was hard to handle and we were all so wet and tired that we would rather lie down and sleep than fool with the cattle.

We thought that after we got started we could sleep in our saddles but we found all the creeks were up and would be impossible to cross for four or five days, so we had to drive the cattle up along the bluff, between Jesse Creek and the bluff.

There was no road or trail so we had to stay awake every minute all day long.

That night we camped on the head of Paul Aiken Creek.

Everything was wet. We wrung the water out of our blankets, put our slickers over them, lay down and went to sleep.

We were a tired bunch and I guess the cattle were nearly as tired as we were, for they bedded down easily and stayed all night without a bit of trouble in spite of the fact that the three herds had been thrown all together just twenty-four hours before.

There had been more wind at Paul Aiken Creek the night before than there had where we had been, for trees were uprooted, and the creek was running bank-full.

Sam Collins, the cook, drove the chuck wagon with Bob Gilstrap in it down the west side of the creek until he got to Sand Creek, which was out of banks all over the bottom lands.

A man named Ed Phillips, who lived on the other side of the creek, had a fishing boat, which he brought across to us. Sam took Bob across in it and then hitched up a team and took him to Elgin, Kansas, to a doctor.

Sam came on back to camp and got in just in time to cook breakfast. After breakfast he fed his team and was ready to go with the chuck wagon when we started the herd in the morning.

Sam told us he had driven all night with no road to follow and in many places through the water of the overflowing creeks with no company but an unconscious man. He just went ahead and trusted God for the outcome.

END OF THE DRIVE

The next morning we swam the cattle across Soldier Creek and put them in the government pasture at the Osage Agency. As they went through the gate the Indian agent, John Miles, and his Indian police counted the cattle; we found we had lost a few but still had forty-nine hundred and eighty head.

The steers brought thirty dollars apiece and the cows eighteen to twenty dollars. The calves brought from one to seven dollars each.

After the bosses got their pay for the herd we made our camp on Soldier Creek.

That evening a couple of the Indian police came out with a pocket full of money; they wanted to play draw poker. We drew our wages and played, and by midnight we still had our wages and four hundred dollars of the policemen's money.

We decided to take our winnings and go up to Elgin and pay Bob's doctor bill, so the next morning eleven of us started for Elgin, Kansas. We got there about two o'clock in the afternoon and found Bob sitting in the doctor's office looking pretty bad but feeling fairly well.

We gave him the wages that Osage Brown had sent him and we paid the doctor what Bob already owed and for another week's treatment, and we still had two hundred and eighty dollars left.

Bob was a full-blooded Cherokee Indian and he didn't talk much. He put his hand up to his bandaged head and looked down at his feet and then at us and said, "Thanks, boys."

With everything thus taken care of, we now started out to do a little celebrating of our own.

A bunch of the boys from the Carpenter Ranch were in town, so we all stayed together and had a lot of fun.

We started at Tom Leahey's store and finished up at a dump down by the railroad tracks. The officers didn't try to stop us but just said, "Go ahead, boys! Paint her a deep crimson."

12 HOLY MOTHER, PRAY FOR US

A NEW JOB

When I got back from the big drive there wasn't anything to do for the Cattlemen's Association right then, so Jonas Swanick and I went to work for Florer and Shaddon who ran the Trading Post at Gray Horse, about twenty- five miles southwest of the Osage Agency.

Our job was breaking wild ponies. We camped by the blacksmith shop and boarded ourselves.

The foreman was John Goodin. He and his family lived in a small frame house on the east bank of Gray Horse Creek about one hundred yards above the blacksmith shop.

The store and other buildings were on the west side of the creek.

The Indian camp and all the Indian lodges were south and west of the store. The milk lot was north of the store.

Jonas and I would saddle the wild broncs and go tearing out on the prairie. There we stayed with them until they were ready to ride. We helped the boys look after the stock, drive the milk cows and cut them into the milk lot.

Then we would go to our camp and have supper.

After supper we would pick out the ponies we were going to ride the next day, rope them and tie them up until the next morning, then loaf around the store until bedtime.

There was always a crowd of Indians at the store.

Many times Jonas and I would go to the Indian lodges nearby and listen to the old men tell their legends.

There were two that I liked best.

Here they are:

****

ON A STAR

After your loved ones die they live on a star so that they can watch over you.

Watch the stars at night and if you look long enough the one where your loved one lives will shine brighter for you than any of the other stars. If you will ask Wah-ken-tucka, the Great Indian Spirit, he will let your loved one send down a message that you can feel in your heart, a message of love and good counsel.

****

Many times I have lain on the ground at night looking up at the stars and after a while one of them seems brighter.

As you look you feel the presence of the loved one on that star. You seem to feel her understanding and love.

You may be planning something that would be the wrong thing to do. As you watch your star, many times you will change your plans, as though you had been guided by an invisible hand.

Try it. You will find your loved one on the brightest star.

****

CURTAINS

Wah-ken-tucka, the Great Indian Spirit, said to the wise men, "I will put a curtain in front of the future to hide all the evils that frighten you, for know you not that you live only in the present moment? When the night comes dream of the future and see if your dream comes true"

Since that day we cannot tell what may happen, for the curtain is before us. But we can paint on it beautiful pictures, not with our hands but with our spirit, and ask the Great Indian Spirit to help us make them come true.

But the curtain rolls up and we cannot see beyond the present.

We can only ask Wah-ken-tucka to look after us, for he alone knows the future.

****

I thought it was a beautiful legend, and I learned to know that it was the right thing to wait overnight when I planned on doing anything rash or violent.

JENNIE

Mrs. Goodin, the foreman's wife, had a younger sister named Jennie. She was a beautiful girl and deeply religious. She was a Catholic and lived her faith constantly.

Jennie was half French and half Osage Indian. She was small and slender and she wore her black hair in a French roll, that is, rolled to one side from the back to the front.

Her features were perfect. God made her as beautiful as woman could be made.

I was in love with Jennie but I worshiped her in silence.

151

You know, you can ride up to a spring and you may find a lovely cardinal flower, brilliant and beautiful, blooming out there all alone, where no one knows of its presence, just beautifying the wilderness where only God knows about it and rewards it for its efforts.

Jennie was like the cardinal: out there in nowhere trying to improve the moral lives of a bunch of us no-good rannies.

She was beautiful and modest and had more real religion than all the rest of us put together.

I was like all the rest of the fellows: ready to back her with both guns!

I was a favorite in the Goodin household. I used to go up to the milk lot and help Mrs. Goodin and Jennie milk. We would take care of the cows, then carry the milk over to the house and put it away. After that we would sit and talk, or sing, until bedtime.

I knew that Jennie liked me and I did not dare to hope for more than that.

CAPTAIN WILLIAM A. "BILL" KNIPE

Captain Bill Knipe was head of the Cattlemen's Association with headquarters in Arkansas City. I was still working for the Association and subject to call at any time.

One day, Jean Townsend, the freighter who hauled freight from Arkansas City, brought me a letter from Captain Knipc telling me to report to him, for orders, at the Gladstone Hotel in Arkansas City.

The next morning I went up to Arkansas City and reported to Captain Knipe. He gave me my orders and a letter of introduction to a Captain Anson down in Texas.

As I was leaving the hotel I asked Captain Knipe if he had any further instructions for me. "No," said the captain, "only, keep your eyes and ears open and your mouth shut!"

I thought that was the best advice I ever had and told him so. He grinned, "Take it, son, and good luck be with you."

He watched me a few minutes, then went back into the hotel shaking his head.

I rode out the east road, crossed the Walnut River and on to Gray Horse Station, thinking of my orders and the method I would use to carry them out.

The next morning I went into the office and drew the wages due me.

John Florer gave me a Stetson hat and two boxes of shells for a bonus. We shook hands and he told me to come back when I finished my job.

I went out to catch my two ponies. I put my pack on old Bowlegs and the saddle on Mollie. Mollie was a white mare with a black mane and tail.

I had raised her from a colt and we understood each other. She was a good runner and a good swimmer, and she would stand all day — almost without moving.

Mollie had no brands and sometimes that helped me out when I was watching cattle thieves. She wasn't a range horse but she sure was a tracker.

I think she knew as much about cattle thieves as I did.

I tied the pack on my pack pony with a diamond hitch and when the weather was cool and there were no flies, I tied him to the tail of the one I rode.

But if the flies were bad and my saddle horse needed his tail to fight them, I tied my pack pony to the saddle horn with about eight feet of rope and let him trot along behind.

When I dismounted I left him tied to the saddle and ground-hitched my riding horse.

I threw the bridle reins down on the ground and went up to the foreman's house to tell the folks good-by.

GOOD-BY TO JENNIE

George Goodin and his wife were on the porch and after talking with them for a few minutes Mrs. Goodin told me that Jennie was in the kitchen.

As I went in she was standing by the worktable looking at me.

"Frank, they tell me you are going away." She walked toward me. "Where are you going?"

"I can't tell you, Jennie, but as soon as I can I will be back."

"If I guess where you are going, will you tell me?"

"I sure will!" I didn't think she had a chance to guess where I was going for it was a closely guarded secret.

I was wrong!

"You are going down to Texas after the Buckley brothers."

"What in the world made you say that? I thought no one knew."

"Well, I heard Mr. Florer bet Mr. Shaddon one hundred dollars that you would come back. Mr. Shaddon bet you wouldn't. Oh, Frank, it nearly killed me." She walked over and laid her little hands on my shoulders and I drew her to me and kissed her.

154

She was the first girl I had ever kissed. She laid her head on my shoulder and sobbed.

Jennie stepped back from me and opening the neck of her dress took out a small silver medallion. It had the image of the Virgin Mary, in gold, upon it, with the inscription, "Holy Mother Pray for Us."

Holding it out to me she said, "Keep it, Frank; it is yours if you will wear it for me."

I promised.

She then took from around her neck a large crucifix. It was made of steel and the cross was a full inch wide and three inches long. The cross bar was an inch wide and about two inches long. The whole thing was heavy silver-plated, with the figure of Christ in gold. Kissing it, she tied it around my neck.

"Now, Frank, this I want you to bring back. Always wear it until we meet again. Know that I am praying for you every day and every hour of the day. Be careful. It would kill me to lose you now."

I kissed her once more and she walked with me out where my ponies were waiting.

I rode down the creek to the Arkansas River. It was low and I crossed at the ford and went on to the Pawnee Agency.

I crossed Black Bear Creek at the rock ford and camped for the night on the south bank where there was plenty of grass for my ponies. Stripping the blankets off my ponies' backs, I staked them out, made some coffee and ate my supper.

Then I lay on my blanket and painted beautiful pictures on the curtain of the future until I fell asleep.

The next morning I started early. I crossed the Cimarron at the Nipps horse ranch on the Burke Norton trail and camped that night in the timber south of the river.

Starting early in the morning and riding hard in a southwest direction, I rode on to complete my mission.

CAPTAIN ANSON

Several days later I arrived at the Rocking Chair outfit in Texas.

Riding up to the yard fence I saw Captain Anson on the gallery.

On the table beside him was a large wooden cracker box.

On one side of the box was the picture of a big parrot and the box was filled with homegrown tobacco. Beside it was a jug and some glasses.

The captain was smoking a long-stemmed clay pipe and greeted me with the old Texas hail, "Light, stranger, and look at your saddle."

I got off my pony and tied her to the fence and went up on the porch and took the chair the captain offered. As I sat down he called a Negro, who came in with a pitcher of water and a glass.

"Wet your whistle," the captain said, pushing the jug and glasses toward me.

"Thanks," I replied, "but I'll take water." I drank heartily—the water was good.

"I always want my whisky first," the captain poured out a drink and swallowed it.

"It's all right," I said, "but I have made a promise not to drink and I am going to keep my word."

"That's all right boy, do it; no hard feelings." The captain turned to Sam, the Negro boy, and told him to take my ponies to the feedlot and put the saddles in the shed.

"Have you ridden far, son?"

"Quite a ways." I watched the boy looking over my ponies as he led them away. "Do you have any work you could set me at for a while?"

"Might be. When the foreman comes in, you can find out. Where you from?"

"The Cherokee Nation. My folks live about twenty miles south of Caney, Kansas."

"How far back is the sheriff?"

I laughed. "I don't know, but I left Captain Knipe in Arkansas City." The captain looked at me keenly and just then the foreman came riding up.

Throwing down his reins he jumped off his horse and came in.

"Hello," he said as he filled a glass with water and drank it.

"Griff," said the captain, "this boy wants work and he says he knows Captain Knipe in Arkansas City.

How long have you known him, son?"

"Quite a while." I handed him Captain Knipe's letter of introduction. He looked at the letter and then at me. Then he opened it.

"Damn their hides!" he cried, handing the letter to Griff, "I told them to send me the best man they had and here they send me a boy hardly dry behind the ears. Do they expect him to do a job that three good men have failed to do?"

Then, looking at me, he said, "Are you damn sure that your name is Frank Eaton and this letter is yours?"

For answer I showed him my United States Deputy Marshal's badge and commission.

"Well," said the captain, "you may be like a singed cat —better than you look. I hope you are, for you will need all you've got. Now, how do you propose to start in?"

"I would like to work as a stray man," I told him. "Don't tell even your own men that I am not a regular hand."

"All right." Turning to Griff, he said: "In the morning cut him out a string and give him the lay of the country.

Don't tell any of the boys anything — only that he is on as a stray man."

A stray man rides to all the different ranches looking for stray cattle from his ranch. In that way I could find out a lot about the country, the cattle and the people, without any questions being asked of me.

The next morning the boys drove in a bunch of ponies and I cut out my string of three and saddled one of them.

Griff, the foreman, rode to the top of a hill with me and showed me the lay of the country and where the other ranches and the water holes were located.

"Now go to it, son. I hope you have better luck than the other fellows they have sent down here.

When you need us we will be ready. There are two trails through the hills that they drive the stolen cattle out on. The trails are easy to block if we only knew when to block them."

Wishing me luck, Griff turned and rode back to the corral.

I rode on to the first water hole, where I looked at the cattle and watered my pony; then on to the first ranch, where I stayed all night.

In the morning I took another route and scouted the trails over which the thieves drove their stolen stock.

I always carried a pair of good field glasses and they saved me many a long ride.

In a week's time I was thoroughly familiar with the whole country and all the ranches. In none of them did I find any men that I thought were guilty of rustling stock.

CATTLE RUSTLERS

One evening I saw in the distance a dust rising and looking through my glasses I made out eight riders. I was standing on a hill overlooking a water hole.

I hid my pony in a patch of brush and watched the eight riders come in and camp at the water hole.

They staked their ponies, ate their supper and bedded down for the night. The brands on their ponies were strange to that part of the country and I thought they would bear watching.

As soon as I could get away without being seen I rode hard for the ranch. Stopping at the bunkhouse I asked Griff to bring my own pony, Mollie.

Mollie was a good night horse and I wanted a pony that could run if it had to.

I went to Captain Anson and told him what I had seen. I gave him a detailed description of the men and of the ponies they were riding.

"By God, that is them!" said the captain. "Get the boys out and we will clean the bunch clear off the face of the earth. You are all right, son." He started for his hat and gun.

"Hold on," I said, "I am going back alone to watch them. When they start gathering the cows I will come in. You have the boys ready and we'll catch them with the cattle. That is all the proof we'll need. There's nothing against them now that we can prove, but if we find them driving off the cattle we will have them dead to rights and they

can't get out of it. We want enough men so that none of the rustlers will get away. I have asked Griff to bring in my own saddle pony because she has no brands on her and she can outrun her own shadow and keep it up as long as there is any need. There won't be any brands in case I have to tell some kind of a story to explain my presence in the locality. You round up all the men you can depend on and have them ready when I come in."

We walked out to where Griff had my white mare.

"Boys," said the captain as I put the saddle on Mollie, "the Buckley's are on the range! Get ready for business! When this boy comes in, get every man out. Fill your rifles and guns and have a good horse ready to ride. We will make this their last trip to these parts."

I rode off into the night. Mollie was fresh and wanted to run but I held her down to a fast fox trot and we covered the ground rapidly.

In about three hours I came to the place where I had hidden my pony in the brush earlier.

Dismounting, I walked to the edge of the brush; and, looking down from the edge of the little hill, I could see that the rustlers' ponies were still where they were when I left. I went back to where I had left Mollie and lay down and went to sleep.

160

WATCHING

At daylight I was up and watched the rustlers eat their breakfast.

Two of them rode out to where a large bunch of cattle were grazing. They rode among the cattle, looking them over, then on to another bunch.

The other men lay around the water hole. They watered their ponies and staked them out again with their saddles on them. Then they lay down until the two riders came in.

It was about ten o'clock in the morning when the two men came in and they all talked for a while. Then all of them mounted, rode up on a timbered hill and camped again. They were in a place where they could see everything that came by but not be seen themselves.

I had not thought of that kind of move. Now I could not leave without their seeing me, yet I didn't want Mollie to stay there without water. If I rode down to the water hole they would

see me. I took my canteen and washed out Mollie's nostrils and, pouring the rest of the water into my hat, let her drink it all up clean. Then I lay down again and watched.

About noon a rider from a nearby ranch came up to the water hole. After watering his pony he rode on through the cattle and over to another bunch.

I wished I could tell him what was going on but didn't dare for fear I would tip off the rustlers.

About an hour by sun they came out of the timber riding down to the water hole, they watered their ponies and had supper.

Then they rode out to the cattle and started them down to the water hole. After letting them drink they started driving them on in a southwest direction.

Waiting until they had gone, I then rode over the hill and headed for the ranch at full speed.

It was almost dark when I arrived and Captain Anson and the boys were getting ready to ride out and look for me. I put my saddle on another pony and we all started back.

"They are heading for the south pass," said Captain Anson. "We can cut through and catch them there." He led the way.

The horse wrangler at the ranch was a boy about thirteen years old. He had his pony ready but the captain told him he was too young and would not let him go. But when we got to the pass the boy joined us.

Captain Anson swore like a bullwhacker but the boy only laughed.

"I am here and I am going to ride right beside Frank. I think I will come out all right. What's the odds if I don't? A fellow only has one time to die and I don't think my time has come yet."

Looking up at me he said, "You don't care, do you, Frank? What are your orders?"

"Well, all I have to say is: shoot first and be sure you don't miss." I hoped he would be able to use that advice.

HERE THEY COME!

We could hear the cattle coming down through the pass.

The captain told Griff to take three of the boys and ride down the ravine and come out ahead of the cattle. They were to get the rustlers' pointers — as we called the front riders — and swing the cattle around.

We were to wait until Griff and the boys had time to get there and start turning the cattle; then we were to go in.

Griff had hardly raised the bank when there was a gunshot from the rustlers, followed by a scattering of the cattle.

The captain and the rest of us went in.

"You and the boy ride to the other side," yelled the captain to me, "and don't let a damned man get away!"

In they went, as fast as their horses could run, shooting at any rider they saw.

There was a bright moon. It was almost light as day.

The boy and I were on the right of the cattle. The captain and his men were on the left.

Griff and his men had stampeded the cattle and killed the pointers and the whole bunch was coming pell-mell through the pass.

The roar of the cattle's hoofs coming down through that canyon fairly shook the ground!

Steers were bawling, men were yelling and shots firing. The dust was so thick we could hardly breathe. The rustler pointers were trampled beyond recognition. Those cattle were stampeding and all we could do was get out of the way.

As the boy and I were getting out of the way of the running cattle we were met by two of the rustlers. They started firing as they came. I felt a heavy blow on my breast that almost knocked me out of the saddle. I caught my balance, and seeing the boy beside me firing steady and true, I straightened up and we shot it out with them.

As the two rustlers toppled off their horses Griff came riding up and asked if we were hurt. The boy answered, "Frank is hit; I saw him sway and nearly fall off his horse."

Griff turned to me, "How bad is it, Frank?"

"I don't think they hurt me much." I didn't know myself what had happened.

Griff went to look for the captain and the rest of the boys.

All our men came through all right. One of Griff's men was hit in the side by the first shot that was fired but it wasn't serious.

The captain had had his hat shot off and it was trampled out of all semblance to a sky piece.

I looked myself over to see what had happened to me.

I had been hit by a bullet that struck the steel crucifix that Jennie had placed around my neck!

The crucifix was broken into two pieces. One piece and the bullet had slid down my pants leg into my boot.

There was a hole in my shirt where the bullet had gone through.

The boys had gathered around and we just sat there and looked!

I'd rather have the prayers of a good woman in a fight like that than half a dozen hot guns: she's talking to Headquarters.

I picked up the pieces of the crucifix and the bullet and put them into my pocket.

THAT JOB WAS DONE

We camped there the rest of the night. In the morning we buried the rustlers in the draw, rounded up their ponies and went back to the ranch.

The captain called to me. "Well, son," he said, "you have done your job and done it well. I will let you take a letter home to Captain Knipe. You had better lay around awhile, for that lump on your wishbone may be worse than you think it is. A few days rest won't hurt you, anyhow. I will have your letter ready tomorrow."

I thanked him but wanted to get home as soon as I could. I was thinking of Jennie and how anxiously she would be waiting. I had been away almost a month.

The letter was ready at last, and I bade them all good-by and started for Arkansas City.

I was on the trail early each morning and rode until late.

At night I lay on the grass and painted beautiful pictures on the curtain of the future. I dreamed of a home in the hills, with a bunch of cattle and ponies, until I fell asleep — to wake early in the morning and ride on.

I made good time and on the evening of the sixth day arrived in Arkansas City.

I got a shave and a new shirt and went up to turn in my letter.

Captain Knipe read it and said, "Frank, this is the best report we have ever had from any of our operatives. You have done well. Now there is nothing further for you at the present time. How much were your expenses?"

"About forty dollars." Captain Knipe gave me the money and added ten more to it. I was very happy.

165

WHO ARE WE TO QUESTION?

Early next morning I was on my way to the Goodins', where Jennie would be waiting for me.

I rode hard and reached the Kaw Agency a little after noon, stopping only to water my pony.

I crossed Beaver Creek and reached Gray Horse before sundown.

I rode up to Goodins', turned my pony loose, and started up the path.

Mr. and Mrs. Goodin were sitting on the porch, but they did not see me until they heard the gate latch. They both rose to their feet and came to the edge of the porch to meet me. Mrs. Goodin was crying when she took my hand and George wiped his eyes and tried to talk; but the only words that came were "Jennie! Jennie!"

"What is wrong with Jennie?" I cried frantically.

Just then a priest stepped out of the door. Father Ponsaloni, a holy and a kindly man, laid his hand on my shoulder and Mrs. Goodin, in a voice broken by weeping, told me, "We buried her three days ago. It was pneumonia. She lived four days."

I sat down on the edge of the porch and buried my head in my hands.

The whole world turned black.

The kindly priest put his hand on my head and said, "She is in heaven, son. Remember that God took her to Himself to live forever in glory and that He does all things for the best."

"That may all be true," I said, "but why would He take one as good and pure as she, who made the whole world around her better, and spare the life of a low gunman? That is more than I can understand." I buried my face in my hands again and cried.

166

The priest said: "My son, who are we to question the acts of the Ruler of the Universe? He can see the motives in the hearts of men. We must accept His divine works for the best."

I had no answer. The curtain of the future had rolled up; the beautiful pictures were all blotted out. I thought I could not face that future.

Mrs. Goodin, Jennie's sister, put her hand on my shoulder and handed me a letter. "Jennie wrote this the day before she died and I promised to give it to you."

I took it eagerly. Tearing the envelope open, I saw the first words: "My Darling Boy ..." I could see no more.

Father Ponsaloni waited a few minutes, then took the letter from my hand and read it to me; every word was like dipping your hand in a spring of cool water and letting it drip off your fingers on a fevered gunshot wound.

****

My Darling Boy, I will not be able to meet you when you come but darling I will be waiting for you in that beautiful land where there is no more parting or strife or sin for Frank, I am dieing. But I am ready but would like to embrace you once more before I go but God knows Best and doeth all things well though we may not see it that way.

But Darling live right be honest and true to yourself and the entire world, as I know you will. Father Ponsiloni administered extreme uncion and just finished. It will be many years before we meet again and there will come other loves to you but in that blessed heaven I will be waiting to welcome you. May the holy Mother and all the saints' guard and keep you.

Good Bye My Darling good Bye

JENNIE

****

I listened silently until he had finished reading and held the letter out to me. I folded it, put it back into the envelope and put it in my breast pocket.

"How will I ever be able to live the life that sainted angel laid out for me?"

"Through prayer, my son," answered the father. "Look for divine help and you can do almost anything."

"Maybe so," I said as I stood up.

"Where is Jennie buried?"

"In the cemetery at the Osage Agency," he told me gently. "I am going there in the morning and will show you."

He walked with me to where my ponies were eating grass and waiting to be unsaddled. "Be brave, my son, and live the way she told you, so you may see her again and be with her forever."

"That is a beautiful thing to think about and if my life work was done I would be there in the morning."

"Not so, my son; that would keep you apart forever. All wounds heal in time. Do as she asked and be a good true man."

The priest had arrived only a few minutes before me and his pony was still standing by the fence. He had come from the St. Mary's Mission, Kansas, where he lived.

We turned our ponies into the feedlot and went into the house.

One of the boys went over to the store to tell Johnnie Florer I was back and he had won his wager from Mr. Shaddon. While he was there he collected a twenty-five-dollar bet of his own from Mr. Shaddon, who had been very sure I would not come back.

That night I lay out under the stars and looked long and earnestly before I found the one I was looking for; then I lay and watched it until I went to sleep.

BRING BACK THE CRUCIFIX

In the morning I started with Father Ponsaloni for the Osage Agency.

On the way I showed him the crucifix broken by the rustler's bullet and the medallion Jennie had given me. I told him what Jennie had said as she placed the crucifix around my neck. "This I want you to bring back to me. Always wear them till we meet again. I will pray for you every day and every hour of the day."

I knew many stories like this had been told — but this had really happened to me.

He listened until I had finished. "You think her prayers saved you?"

"Of course," I answered, "God listens to people such as she was."

"Such as she is, you mean," said Father Ponsaloni, "for she is only changed from mortal to immortal. She is still interceding for you."

"I hope so. I will need it. Things look very dark ahead for me. The trail doesn't seem worth the riding."

"That is not what she told you in her letter and no man ever went wrong who followed the advice of a good woman who loved him. Your sorrow is fresh and hard to bear, but God knows all these things, my son, and He will help you if you trust in Him."

We crossed Bird Creek and rode up past Scotty McGloufing's place and on up the hill to the cemetery. We let our ponies graze and went out to the new mound the priest showed me.

169

Kneeling down at the head of the grave I dug a hole as deep as I could reach with my hand; and in it I put the broken crucifix. Then I filled up the hole and packed the earth firmly around it.

I had brought the crucifix back to Jennie

There on my knees at the head of Jennie's grave I thanked the priest for his words of comfort, and he laid his hand on my head and prayed for me and blessed me.

Then, turning back to his pony, Father Ponsaloni mounted and rode away, leaving me alone.

I lay on the ground by Jennie's grave until dark.

Again I watched the stars come out. And now my star was bright and beautiful.

13 GRAY HORSE STATION

ARCHIE STRATTON

I was back at Gray Horse Station riding for Florer and Shaddon, staying at the bunkhouse with the rest of the boys.

One day I was riding down the Arkansas River, along the north bank below the mouth of Gray Horse Creek, looking for some ponies, and I rode up by Charlie Drum's place.

Charlie was an Indian chief. His name in the Osage language was Sha-ka-lom-pa. There were some Pawnee Indians camped there visiting him.

I had just passed Charlie's place when I met Archie Stratton. Archie said the Indian agent had sent him down to Charlie Drum's to do a little work.

The next day I was back down that way looking after the same bunch of ponies and thought I'd stop to see if Archie had finished his job.

I asked Charlie Drum where Archie was and he said he had not seen him. I told him I had met Archie the day before coming down there, but the old Indian insisted he hadn't come.

I knew there was something wrong, for Archie was in sight of Charlie's house when I had seen him and I knew he had gone there.

So after rounding up the ponies I went back up to the camp and told the boys about it.

The next day Buckskin Pete, Jonas Swanick and I went down to see what had happened to Archie.

There was a well in the yard and as we rode up to get a drink of water, Charlie hollered to us, "Get away from that well and let it alone. A dog jumped into the well and drowned and we never got him out."

Now, by this time we were close enough to the well to smell something dead, and because a dead dog doesn't smell like a dead human being, we knew we weren't smelling a dead dog.

Just then, however, about a dozen Indians came out with their rifles pointed at us so we rode off.

The boys at our camp talked it over and decided on a plan — but we needed help so we sent up to Carpenter's ranch and got some of the boys to come down to help us.

They pretended they had come down just to visit us and they brought along some other boys to visit and play cards with us.

Well, they all wanted to go with us but somebody had to stay at the camp and provide an alibi for those of us who left, for if there was trouble the Indian agent would investigate.

We took five grains of corn apiece and played freeze-out draw poker, and the first four fellows that went broke had to stay at the camp, visit around at the store and make enough noise to give an alibi for all of us, so the foreman would think we were all there.

The rest of us got on our ponies and rode out the back way to Charlie Drum's place.

The Pawnee Indians had left and Charlie Drum had gone along with them. The rest of the Indians who lived on the place were asleep in the lodges a little distance from Charlie's lodge, where the well was.

Some of the boys stood guard while some of the rest of us went down into the well.

We soon found Archie's body and handed him up to the boys who were waiting.

Then we climbed out of the well.

We looked him over to see what had happened.

Archie had been chopped in the head with an ax and then shot through the throat.

We all saw red. Archie was our friend.

We got on our horses and rode down through the Indian lodges. We had to be a little careful, for there were, women and children there that we didn't want to hurt; so we just set the lodges afire, and thus could sec who to shoot at.

Those Indians didn't have time to put out the fire for running! The ones that didn't get into the brush got into the Happy Hunting Ground.

We took Archie up on the hill and buried him.

He had been killed for the money he carried, for there was no money on him and we knew he had had around three hundred dollars.

After we had taken care of Archie we rode away and we all got back into camp before daylight.

Some of the Indians who got away went to the Indian agent and told him what had happened.

The Indian agent came out to the trading post with his Indian police and asked Johnnie Florer and the ranch foreman if they knew where the boys had been that night.

Both of them said yes, the boys had all been right there in camp all night.

Then the Indian agent came and asked us, and, of course, we had been there.

The Indian women wouldn't talk and none of the braves wanted to either. They hadn't been able to see who had attacked them, for they had been running like the devil.

Even in those days you had to prove a man guilty and nobody was guilty of anything.

Those Indians sure gave us a wide road after that.

But Charlie Drum, old Chief Sha-ka-lom-pa, didn't get his until later — but that's another story.

FUN AT THE RACES

There was a whisky peddler by the name of Lee West who had borrowed fifty dollars from me at Christmas time to start his whisky business.

When I saw him at Arkansas City at the horse races on the Fourth of July, he paid it back.

In the meantime he had bought two good farms in the Walnut River bottom and had five thousand dollars in the bank. He had his pockets full of money and was spending freely.

Ed Lewis, foreman at the Hackelford Ranch, and some of his boys had come over from Beaver Creek for the races.

There was a large crowd and we were all having a good time.

Some shorthorn cowpunchers from up in Kansas wanted everyone to think they were bad men, but who were really just common "grasshopper grangers," were there, too.

Ed Lewis and I took their guns away from them and gave them to the city marshal. We were afraid the damn fools might try to draw on

174

someone and get themselves killed — for the whole lot was drinking, and hunting for someone they could run a bluff on.

There was a young farmer who was winning a lot of money on the races and some of the dance-hall girls were trying to attract his attention and get some of his cash. But he was too busy to bother with them and would just buy them a drink and go away and leave them.

Finally one of them threw her arms around his neck and said, "Oh, honey, let me kiss you for your mother."

Pushing her away he said angrily, "Damn you, my mother is a decent woman."

That started it.

All six of the "grasshopper grangers" piled on him and the girl pulled off her shoe and beat him in the face with the heel.

Sime Love, an old trail boss, was standing a short distance away and had seen all that happened.

He came charging in like a mad bull. He had two guns on but never touched either of them. He was a large man, over six feet tall and weighing over two hundred pounds, and what he did to those six "grasshopper grangers" was sure plenty!

He got them all down at the same time and lifted the farmer boy and handed him to me, then turned his attention to his opponents.

One of them wiped the blood from his face and said, "It's all right, Sime, but if I had a gun there would be some new faces in hell for breakfast!"

Sime drew his left-hand gun and holding it by the barrel reached it out to him saying, "Here is a better gun than you ever had. Take it and show me how you can use it, you cowardly son of a bitch!"

Now, that term, when spoken in earnest, was like an Indian's gobble. It meant death!

The fellow didn't take the gun. Sime offered it to each of the six men and none of them took it. Then the marshal, who was standing nearby, said, "Put it up, Sime, they are too yellow to fool with." And he took the six shorthorns and put them into the cooler for the rest of the celebration.

LEE WEST

After the fight Lee West asked me where I was working and I told him Jonas Swanick and I were riding broncs for Florer and Shaddon.

Lee said he was coming down in a few days with some whisky and would bring me a gallon of good stuff.

The whisky he sold to the Indians was made this way: he would send to M. Landuar and Company, Joplin, Missouri, and get ten gallons of alcohol.

He would then put one pint of alcohol into a gallon jug and pour in two tablespoons full of burnt-sugar water. Then he would fill the rest of the jug with water.

Since he paid only one dollar and seventy-five cents per gallon for the alcohol and sold each gallon jug for from twenty-five to forty dollars, he was doing all right.

A few days after the races Lee came out to Gray Horse Station with four packhorses loaded down.

He hid the whisky and took the horses up to Maple City and left them with a friend, then he came back to sell out.

AN UNPOPULAR DEPUTY

Jonas and I each had a wild bronc and were pulling leather, hard, when, riding around the point of a hill north of the store, we saw Lee coming toward us.

He had our gallon and one for Johnnie Florer on his horse and told us to take Florer's jug in to the store for him.

"We can't do it, Lee," we told him, "Charlie Evenhoe is at the store right now, looking for you."

Charlie was a Deputy United States Marshal, and was hunting for trouble.

"Good," said Lee. "You ride down there and tell him you saw me here. Pretend to be drunk so he won't make you come back with him. Then let him come out and catch me if he can."

We hid the whisky in the brush. Reeling in our saddles and yelling like the devil on a tear, pretending to be drunk, we rode down to the store where Charlie was standing on the porch talking to Johnnie Florer.

"What the hell is the matter mit dem damn fools?" asked Charlie.

"They must be drunk," said Johnnie. He knew better, but he didn't like a Dutchman anyway, especially Charlie, who was a most unpopular person in those parts.

In those days some of the officers were as bad as the men they hunted. Charlie was always looking for trouble and a little too quick to take advantage of his position.

He came out to where we were sitting on our broncs. "Say, poys," he said, "vare did you get dot vhisky?"

"Lee West set 'em up to us," Jonas told him, while I leaned over the far side of my horse and pretended to be sick.

"Lee West! Vare is he?" cried Charlie, as he grabbed his shotgun and put on his hat.

"We just left him around the hill," said Jonas.

Charlie jumped on his little pack mule and started out.

When he got out of hearing we told Johnnie Florer that he had something coming, and we rode off to bring in the jugs we had hidden.

We wanted to see how Charlie and Lee came out so we rode to the top of the hill. Staying in the timber where we would not be seen, we sat on our broncs and waited.

Charlie came around the hill looking in all directions for his man.

As he got to the center of a big patch of bare alkali ground Lee raised up out of the grass, a few yards away, and covered him with his Winchester, telling him to drop his shotgun and ride toward him.

The distance between the two men was a little too far for Charlie's shotgun and he knew that Lee was a dead shot with the Winchester, so he slid the shotgun off the mule and rode out to where Lee was standing with his gun aimed right at him.

When he got within about ten steps of him Lee told him to stop and, stooping down, he picked up a half-gallon jug and a pigging string and walked over to where Charlie sat on the mule.

"Why, hello, Charlie," he said, just as though it was the first time he had seen him, "it's been a long time since we met, and now, here we are, out here all alone with no one to bother us. Let's have a drink!" He pulled the cork from the jug, and, after taking a drink, handed it to Charlie.

"Drink hearty," he said and turned the muzzle of his rifle on Charlie, who took the jug and drank a small swallow.

"Oh, come now, don't be bashful! Drink hearty and deep or something might happen to you."

Charlie drank like a thirsty horse.

"Now, that's better," said Lee. "For fear your mule might throw you I will just fasten you on."

He tied Charlie's feet together under the mule's belly.

"Now, I don't think he can throw you; let's have another drink! Now, now, take a good one!" Charlie glared at him but the rifle was looking right at his belt so he took another drink.

Hanging the jug on Charlie's saddle, Lee took the mule's lead rope and led him back to where Charlie had dropped his shotgun. Throwing out the shells, he jammed the muzzle of the gun in the soft ground until the barrel was half full of dirt, then he stuck it into the ground and left it there.

Taking the jug and turning to Charlie, he made him drink as long as he could hold his breath.

Then he led the mule out where his own horse was hidden in the bushes.

Leading the mule with Charlie on him, Lee started for the store.

There were about fifty lodges of Indians camped on the prairie south of the store and they all came out to watch.

Lee led the mule down to the hitch-rack in front of the store and called to Johnnie Florer.

Johnnie came out and they both took a drink and Lee told him to take good care of Charlie. Lee was afraid, he said, that Charlie might have drunk too much and Lee didn't want anything to happen to any of his drinking companions.

179

Then he gave Johnnie the lead rope.

Lee mounted his horse and rode up through the Indian lodges, telling the Indians where to meet him to get their whisky.

From there he rode on out to the timber on Salt Creek.

About this time Jonas and I came in, bringing Johnnie's jug out of hiding, along with our own. Both were filled with a brand called "Singer's Special Reserve."

Jonas and I untied Charlie's feet and took him into the barn but he didn't sober up for two days.

Then Johnnie gave him a drink and a lot of strong black coffee and he rode off for the Indian agency.

TIME CATCHES UP

When Lee West had sold out all his whisky he went back to Arkansas City to order another load.

He didn't sell that one, though, because he got on a big drunk while he was in Arkansas City and shot up the town. After he ran the night watchman out of town he started for the Nation, the Indian Territory.

He was crossing the river on the south bridge when he probably happened to remember he had not taken a shot at Captain Knipe, so he turned around and started back to town.

However, in the meantime, the night watchman had hidden himself in the willows at the end of the bridge.

As Lee came along, riding slowly, the night watchman put two loads of buckshot into him, and then ran. Lee fell off his pony.

Apparently thinking his assailant would come back to finish him off, he twisted around, and got the barrel of his Winchester across his leg to steady it, for he was too far gone to hold it up.

Cocking it, he lay there and waited.

That's the way they found him in the morning, dead and stiff, but ready for action to his last breath.

14 THE LAST MAN

ON THE TRAIL AGAIN

IT was late summer, or early fall, 1881, when I heard that Wyley Campsey was out in West Texas.

Wyley Campsey! The last of the six men who had murdered my father so ruthlessly . . . All the rest had been accounted for.

It seemed like a long time ago.

I was almost twenty-one years old now, but nothing had changed except that there was only one man now instead of six.

Until the last man had been brought to justice my job was still unfinished.

I went in to see Johnnie Florer, drew my pay, and got ready for the trip to Texas.

In a couple of days I saddled up old Bowlegs and was ready to start.

I went first to Arkansas City where I told my plan to Captain Knipe, who gave me a letter from the Cattlemen's Association and wished me luck.

There were weeks in the saddle when the days and the nights were just the same.

The prairie nights were bright. Even when the moon was down the sky was filled with stars and always the one star brighter than all the others.

Sometimes I spread my blanket on the ground for a few hours' rest at night. When the trail was easy to follow I slept in the saddle, with the reins loose, and let my pony lead the way.

183

After several weeks of riding I finally arrived in a small settlement known as Ragtown, only to find that my man had got into trouble there, and left.

It was hard to track a man in that part of the country in those days. Probably no one knew where Wyley Campsey had gone, but if they did, they were not telling.

After trying for over a week I was about to give up and go home when a chance remark I over-heard put me back on Wyley's trail.

Finally I learned he had gone to Albuquerque, New Mexico, so I hit the trail again.

Days of sand and burning sun, but the nights cool and beautiful . . . There is no sky like the desert sky at night, the pretty blue clouds and the little white puffs, the star-light casting twisted shadows of the cactus. I loved the stars. They looked so close I could almost reach out and touch them.

And there was always Jennie's star. Many times I could feel her help and loving presence.

At last I left the desert and took a winding trail over the mountains.

On the afternoon of the ninth day I rode into Albuquerque, tired and dusty.

Albuquerque, New Mexico

I cleaned up myself the best I could and started out to look the town over.

PAT GARRETT

I had stopped in one saloon and was coming out of the second one when I noticed a tall man with a heavy mustache standing by the door.

As I started down the street he started right behind me. I turned around and met him.

"Stranger," I said, "you seem to be following me. Is there any information I can give you?"

"Well, yes, there is," said the man, with a Western drawl. "When a young fellow comes into town riding as good an outfit as you have, with a Winchester under his leg and two guns on, when he goes into every dance hall and saloon in town and doesn't take a drink or have anything to do with the girls, he naturally excites a lot of curiosity."

I grinned. "Well," I said, "my name is Frank Eaton, my home is on Sand Creek in Cooweescoowee District in the Cherokee Nation, Indian

185

Territory. I am a rider for the Cattlemen's Association and am in line of duty. Now is there anything more?"

The man smiled. "My name is Pat Garrett," he said, "I am an officer, I have heard of you and am glad to meet you."

We shook hands and he said, "Let's go in and drink something."

This was during the time known as "the Lincoln County War," in New Mexico. I knew Pat Garrett as the well- to-do rancher who, at the risk of his own life, had taken the job of sheriff and was trying to establish a semblance of law and order, so that honest men might live in bloody Lincoln County.

I had the greatest respect for him.

"I don't drink," I told him, "but I will go in with you."

THE END OF THE TRAIL

We walked down the street and went into the next saloon.

As we came up to the bar and the bartender came up to wait on us, I had to look only once. This was the end of the trail. My job was almost finished. Before me stood the last man, Wyley Campsey!

Garrett called for a drink and paid for it.

Laying his hand on my shoulder he walked out with me. "Don't lie to me, boy," he said, "I know you are after a man."

"Yes. What's more, I have found him. It's that damned bartender, and I'm going to get him!"

"Wait, son," said Garrett, "he is a bad hombre, he has been in a lot of trouble, and has two of the fastest gunmen in Lincoln County for his bodyguards."

I threw back my head and laughed. "I don't care if he has the whole United States Army for bodyguards. He or I will hear the cook call breakfast in hell. Let's go Pat and I will tell you why I am after him."

We went into a restaurant and sat down at an out-of-the-way table in the back. There were no other customers, so we could talk.

I told him the story of my father's murder.

How I had carried in my heart, all these years, the picture of my father lying in the doorway, a man standing over his body, emptying his gun into my father's lifeless form.

How I had fallen on my father's body, screaming, only to be pulled away, brutally struck with a riding whip and kicked across the room.

187

Then I told him the words of Mose Beaman. I could almost hear Mose saying, "May an old man's curse be upon you if you do not try to avenge your father. You must never stop until the last man has been accounted for."

I told Pat Garrett of the years that followed, of learning how to shoot, of how all the other killers had been brought to justice and how I felt, now that I was face to face with the last man, Wyley Campsey, the bartender in the saloon next door.

I showed Pat Garrett my Deputy United States Marshal badge and commission and my letter from Captain Knipe of the Cattlemen's Association.

I told him of the murder and thieving of the gang in the Cherokee Nation and how, with the help of the Lighthorsemen, we had cleaned them out; I told him, too, that Wyley was wanted for the murder of an officer at Vian in the Indian Territory.

As Pat Garrett listened he seemed to be weighing every word.

When I had finished he said, "This is something you had better not tackle alone. You know I cannot allow another killing if I can prevent it."

"You can't prevent this one and if you think you can, right now is as good a time to start as you will ever have." I was ready to go for my guns.

"Hold on, son," he said, "you got me wrong. I only meant that you had better let me go in and try to arrest him."

"Oh, no, that man will never submit to arrest. He knows he will hang. Any man would rather die with his gun in his hand."

"You may be right, son, but how are you going to handle this one?"

"Easy enough," I told him, "when you see me ride down and tie my horse in front of that place you go uptown, and come back after the fireworks. It won't be long. I know he is fast but I think I am faster."

"What about the two men, his bodyguards?"

"If they want to take chips in another man's game I guess they will have to play them, that's all. I hope they don't, for they might lose and that would complicate matters for me with the local police."

"Don't worry, son," said Garrett, "there will be no trouble on that score. The thing that worries me is that maybe you have overplayed your hand. Three to one is a hard game and heavy odds."

"I'll risk it and guess we had better be getting busy."

We arose from the table, I paid the bill and we went out on the street.

"Well, son, I like your nerve and wish you the best of luck."

"Thank you, sir, you sure are a man." We shook hands and parted.

I went to the livery barn, saddled my pony and paid the bill.

Then I mounted and rode down the street to the saloon where I had seen Wyley Campsey.

I ground tied old Bowlegs a little to one side of the door so that if any stray shots came through the door they would not hit him.

Working my guns to make sure they were loose in the holsters, I walked through the crowd and stopped at the bar.

"What do you want, kid?" asked Wyley as I stood in front of him.

"I just want you, Wyley."

We were about four feet apart with nothing but the bar between us.

Wyley looked at his two guards. They showed a lack of war wisdom for they came to him instead of staying where they were. That move put all of them in a bunch right under my eyes and close to me.

"Want me? What do you mean?" asked Wyley, flanked by his two gunmen.

"Don't you remember me, Wyley?"

"I never saw you before!"

"Oh yes, you have! It was the night you killed my father! I am Frank Eaton, remember? Fill your hand, you son of a bitch!"

All three of them went for their guns.

Wyley got his to the top of the bar but went down with two forty-fives through his heart.

The guards were lightning on the draw. One of them went down without firing a shot but the other one got me in the leg and again in the

left arm, knocking one of my guns out of my hand, before he went down.

There was a wild stampede among the bystanders when the shooting started, but it was finished before any of them got out the door.

Looking over the bar to be sure there was no need for further action I started for the door and ran right into Pat Garrett. He had been standing in the door looking in.

"How bad are you hit, son?" he asked.

"Not so bad but what I can ride if you will help me onto my horse."

He helped me into the saddle.

"You have lost one of your guns," he said. "Here's another one." He stuck a long gun in my empty holster saying, "After you have ridden a few miles you will see a house off to your right. Go in there and tell them that I sent you. They will dress your wounds and keep you until you are able to go on. They are friends of mine and fine people."

I thanked him and galloped out of town.

FRIENDS

A little later I rode up to the house Pat Garrett had told me about. I hailed and a boy about fourteen years old came to the door.

"Pat Garrett told me to stop here and have some hurts I got tonight tied up."

"All right," he said, "come on in. I will look after your horse while Mother looks after you. Dad will be back from town pretty soon and he will help. My God, man! You are bleeding like hell!"

I staggered into the house and as I sat down heard a horseman ride up outside. The boy went out to meet him and they came in together.

"Hello, son," said the man, "I see you got here all right. Now, let's look at those wounds. Madge, bring a pan of water and some cloth for bandages."

The lady brought the water and bandages and he began dressing the wounds.

"Say, you are a lucky cuss," he said, "I saw that fight and you sure handled your guns rapid."

He took some dressing out of his pocket. "Pat told me he sent you here and he sent this out to you. He would have come along but thought he better look after things in town and help pick up the pieces. The boys were drinking your health and some of them were getting noisy. There now! That arm will be as good as new in a little while. Let's see about the leg." He looked at it closely and then exclaimed, "Why, son, the bullet hardly buried itself. Here it is right under the skin. Can you stand to let me cut it out?"

"Sure," I said, "go ahead."

In a moment he had the bullet in his hand. "A thirty- eight," he said. "That came from Dan's gun, and it hit something and glanced off before it hit you. I was watching close and I thought you fired first, but you didn't."

The boy came in with my Winchester and stood it up in the corner. "I thought you might want it handy," he said.

Turning to the man he asked, "Did you see the fight, Dad?"

I had not realized before that this was the man who lived there.

"I sure did and it was a dandy," he said, "but it was all over almost before it had begun. This fellow shot hell out of the three of them and has only these two little hurts to show for it."

Then looking intently at me he asked, "Say, pardner, what was it you said to Wyley Campsey before you told him to fill his hand? I was listening but I didn't get it."

I told them the whole story and when I had finished he said, "I knew he was bad. I'm glad you got them all. They had killed two miners in that saloon and there was talk it was for the money the miners carried. There was no one else in the place when it happened and they all three swore the miners were killed in a gambling fight. They got out of it but there was some talk of lynching them. But the boys won't have to lynch them now; they are all done for."

He turned to the boy, "Come on, son, and help me pull this boy's boots off and get him bedded down for the night. He must be tired and weak, for he has lost a lot of blood."

In a few minutes I went sound asleep.

MORNING

I woke in the morning to hear the man kindling a fire in the kitchen and the boy coming from the spring with a bucket of water.

The woman came through the room and stopped and asked how I felt. I assured her I was all right and got up and limped down to the horse lot to see if old Bowlegs had been cared for.

The boy had fed the horses and Bowlegs was eating with the rest of them. I went back to the house and got ready for breakfast.

After breakfast I began preparing to go on but the man wouldn't listen to my leaving.

"I want to look after you for a while," he said. "You need to rest and are more than welcome to anything we can do for you. That leg might give you trouble if you went to riding now."

He dressed my wounds again.

I was looking at the gun Pat Garrett had put in my holster. It was a Colt forty-four with an eight-inch barrel and very easy on the trigger end; an almost perfect shooting iron.

Pat's friend looked at the gun and said, "Pat told me he gave you the gun; you're mighty lucky. That's the gun Pat used when he killed Billy the Kid!"

I looked at the gun again with more interest than I had before.

I stayed there at the home of Pat Garrett's friend for almost a week and he dressed my wounds every day.

Then I started back home.

I rode the same trail, under the same sun by day and slept under the same stars at night, watching them come out one by one until I found my star.

Everything was just the same. . . except my world!

The great task of my life was finished. My father's death was avenged. All his murderers were accounted for, even "the last man."

I went back to Arkansas City and made my report to Captain Knipe.

15 ROLLA GOODNIGHT

MOTHER ALWAYS PRAYED

I WENT back to Gray Horse Station and a few days after I arrived a rider came from my old home down on Sand Creek saying Mother was very sick, so I got on my pony and went back with him.

I got home only about an hour before Mother died but she knew me and was glad to see me. She died in childbirth and was only forty-two years old.

They used to say that women who died in child-birth went straight to heaven and I know my mother did.

It was a great grief to her that I took the trail of my father's killers.

She always said, "Leave them to God, He will punish them."

She was afraid I would meet the same end that my father did at the hands of the same men. But the code of the land was different in those days, and my stepfather felt as I did so Mother finally let me go. But she always worried and she always prayed.

We buried her in the Stokes Cemetery in the bend of a big hill about a mile west of the Caney River, northwest of where the city of Bartlesville now stands.

The cemetery was on a little rise all covered with grass, wild violets and primroses. It was a pretty place for Mother to be and I tried to think about it that way.

After Mother's funeral I went down east of the Caney River and was riding for Clem Rogers — Will Rogers's father — when I got orders to

195

report to Captain Knipe at Arkansas City to go on a job for the Cattlemen's Association.

This was early in the year 1882.

A BUDDY

I went up the west trail and stopped all night at the Witherspoon Ranch on Salt Fork.

The horse wrangler at the ranch was a tall rangy boy with sandy hair and honest blue-gray eyes. He was just a boy, younger than I, but he had been on his own for a long time. His name was Rolla Goodnight.

We liked each other and were friends from the start.

I told Rolla I had a letter from the Cattlemen's Association to report to Captain Knipe and I thought they were going to send me to Texas. I asked Rolla to go along.

He said that, some time before, his uncle, Colonel Charles Goodnight, had sent word for him to come down to his ranch in Texas and he would give him a job, so Rolla decided to go with me.

I had an uncle down there, too, Nick Eaton, my father's brother.

Uncle Nick had a cattle ranch on Running Water Creek at that time and he and Colonel Goodnight were friends.

So Rolla and I planned to stay in Texas if we found work.

The next morning Rolla drew his wages and we started for Arkansas City. I reported to Captain Knipe and got my letter; and just as I had thought, it was to take me to Texas.

Rolla and I bought a couple of new shirts, three hundred cartridges for our guns and a dime's worth of salt and started for Texas across the open country.

It was early in the summer, 1882; the creeks and rivers were all running full and deer bringing their young.

The young prairie chickens were about as big as quail — fine eating they were too, and easy to get.

When we reached the Chikaskia River, it was high and we had to swim; and after we got out of the water, we discovered nearly all our salt had washed away.

When we swam the Salt Fork and the Cimarron River, we lost the rest of the salt and had to eat our meat straight, but we didn't care.

We would shoot a deer or antelope and cut off the two hindquarters and tie them on behind our saddle.

When we camped we would cut off some meat and roast it, on a stick, over the campfire. That was supper, and breakfast was the same.

We didn't stop for dinner.

We were in no hurry and never crowded our ponies, but when we found a good place we camped and let our ponies eat. We would lie on the grass and talk.

If there was a good fishing hole we would fish and roast the fish we caught.

When the ponies stopped eating we would ride on again.

Neither of us had ever had a buddy and that was the beginning of a friendship that has lasted almost seventy years and grows warmer as the years pass.

Rolla lives down at Guthrie, Oklahoma, about thirty miles from here, and we see each other often, always ride together at rodeos and in the parades.

In those days we were just two carefree boys having a good time, never knowing at what hour a band of Indians or outlaws might attack but always ready.

If Indians had jumped us they would have had a fight on their hands, for we were both experts with our shooting irons and there would have been mourning in the Indian lodges when the news came in.

There was one thing we had a lot of fun about. Rolla's father thought he was too reckless and always told him he would surely die with his boots on, so when things looked bad Rolla always pulled off his boots. He said he was going to make the old man out a liar if he could.

He explained this to me as he tied his boots to the back of his saddle while we were getting ready to swim the North Canadian River. The river was bank-full, with whirlpools everywhere, and we knew about the quicksand.

It did look like a desperate venture, but we had good swimming ponies.

We made it all right. We stopped on the far side and shook the sand out of our clothes, and Rolla put his boots on.

SMOKE MEANS PEOPLE

We were riding down an old buffalo trail heading southwest when we saw a column of smoke off to the west.

We stopped to watch it, for smoke meant there were others in the neighborhood and we did not want to run into anything unprepared.

"There is too much smoke for a campfire," said Rolla, "and it isn't right for an Indian lodge. It looks like a big branding fire or a small house or tent."

"We've been out of biscuits for over a week now and there might be some over there. What do you think? Aren't you getting tired of a straight meat diet?" I asked.

"Well, it's only about six or eight miles over there," said Rolla.

So we decided to go.

We started in the direction of the smoke, riding in the low places so that we would not be too easily seen and keeping a sharp lookout for an ambush.

It was farther than we thought and the smoke had died out before we rode carefully to the top of the ridge and looked down at the scene before us.

MARAUDING INDIANS

In the embers of the fire were the irons of a burned wagon.

On the ground were the bodies of a man, a woman and a little yellow-haired girl about five years old. They had been killed and scalped by Indians, who had left only their mangled bodies.

We found an old shovel and buried them there and piled the hot irons of the wagon on top of the graves to keep the wolves away.

Then we started riding in a circle around the place to cut signs. That means to find signs — and the way we did it was to start at the center and ride around, riding in a larger circle each time around.

We found there were six or seven Indians in the band and as there was no sign of a fight they must have surprised the travelers and killed them before they had a chance to defend themselves.

The trail of the marauders led off in a southwest direction and we followed it without a word.

We rode hard and as our horses were fresh and the Indians did not expect pursuit we gained rapidly.

It was a bright moonlight night and a little before midnight we came over a rise and saw the outline of ponies grazing.

Dismounting, we took our Winchesters and crept forward to investigate.

We saw the forms of the Indians lying around the embers of their campfire; one of them was sitting up to keep watch.

As we crawled closer I felt Rolla touch me and turning saw his foot stuck out for me to pull off his boot.

We laid both boots together and started on again.

When we got about twenty feet from the Indians we laid down our Winchesters and drew a gun in each hand.

We picked out our men so we would not be aiming at the same ones.

Rising cautiously to our feet we gave a loud yell and went in shooting.

The Indians fired back but they were bad shots and missed us slick and clean.

We had planned to save the one who had the scalp of the little girl and tie him up for the wolves to eat but he put up such a fight we had to kill him along with the rest of them.

Rolla chunked up the fire and started to pick the sand burs out of his feet while I brought in our ponies and Winchesters along with Rolla's boots.

We took the scalps of the man, woman and the little yellow-haired girl off the belts of the dead Indians and buried them, leaving a cross to mark the place.

The bodies of the dead Cheyennes we left for the wolves and the buzzards to eat.

We took the firearms and other things belonging to the Indians and piled them up beside the bodies.

Turning their ponies loose, we let them go back to their camp with the death mark on each one.

The death mark was made by dipping the hand in blood and making a print of the hand on the pony's shoulder.

We watched the ponies lope away and knew the Indians would wonder who it was that knew, so well, the death mark.

"Well," I said, "we better get out of here or there will be two more ponies with the death mark on their shoulders."

As we rode away the fresh clean dawn of another day was breaking over the little rise in the prairie.

But a column of buzzards was wheeling around in the sky above.

THE MULESHOE OUTFIT

As we went through Mobeetie, Texas, we saw a boy in a saloon who had been shot in a fight.

Rolla and I took him outside and laid him in the shade; he was dying. He asked me to mail a letter to his mother. I put it in my pocket and we rode on.

The next day we arrived at the Muleshoe Outfit, where I had been sent by Captain Knipe. We got on as stray men without telling the foreman who I was, and we had been working almost a week before I gave him my letter from Captain Knipe telling him we had been sent to get some cattle rustlers.

One day as we rode up on a little hill where we could look out over the prairie with our field glasses, we could see six or eight unknown riders among the cattle.

There were Spanish brands on their horses, and Mexican saddles. The horses were good; the men were well armed, and were working like experienced cowhands.

We knew they were from across the border.

While we were watching, two other strange riders came up behind us and were right on top of us before we heard them.

They were from the same bunch as the men below and they asked us what we were doing there.

We always had a story fixed up, so we used it then.

We told them we were watching the men below and if they were officers they would never take us alive because we'd just as well die there as at the end of a rope.

It worked!

They laughed and put their guns back in the holsters and asked us to go down to the camp and eat with them. Apparently they thought us only a couple of scared kids, so we went.

While we were all sitting around talking I remembered the letter the dying boy had given me on the way down, and took it out of my pocket. It was addressed to his mother in Austin, Texas.

One of the men said he knew the boy well and that was his handwriting. He thought he better not take the letter, for it might be some time before he could give it to her.

I thought it might be, too, so I told him I would mail it at the ranch.

The men were friendly and not at all suspicious of us, but we wanted to get away so we acted scared and after supper we got on our horses and rode away.

As soon as we were out of their sight we headed for the ranch as fast as our horses would go.

When we described the men to the foreman, he knew the gang and sent word to all the other ranchers.

The men from the nearby ranches gathered that night; but the rustlers hadn't done anything yet. They had been looking over the cattle and picking out the ones they wanted.

The next day they started cutting them out and driving them down by themselves.

They had the very best ones: four-year-old steers, with plenty of beef and good long legs so they could travel.

The rustlers drifted the cattle toward the trail.

Some of our boys were waiting for them on the trail and the rest of us were on the flanks.

When they started down the trail they began to travel faster — and ran right into us.

We turned the cattle and they stampeded right back.

There was a fierce battle. We lost four men and two others were badly wounded, but that was the end of the Mexican cattle rustlers.

COLONEL CHARLES GOODNIGHT

I sent a letter to Captain Knipe telling him the details of the job at the Muleshoe.

Then Rolla and I headed for the Goodnight ranch, the well-known J A Ranch.

It was about a week later when we rode into Palo Duro where Colonel Charles Goodnight had his headquarters —Rolla's Uncle Charlie, who gave us both jobs.

It was late in the summer, 1882, and they were just starting a big fall round up.

Nick Eaton, my father's brother, who had a ranch up on Running Water Creek, was there taking part in the roundup. We started right in gathering cattle.

Comanche Pool had leased some land up in the northwestern part of the Indian Territory, to start a ranch, and Colonel Goodnight had sold him some she-stuff to raise from.

Nick Eaton also threw in a few hundred head and Deaf Smith was there to receive and pay for them.

They drove them up the trail to the Indian Territory and Colonel Goodnight stayed right with his cowhands helping until the cattle were trail-broke and off the home range.

Then, since he had his cattle rounded up, he took a drove of steers up the trail and sold them in the Kansas market.

When the colonel got back home he went to looking for cattle rustlers. He hated a cow thief worse than the devil hates holy water. Besides, none of the boys was allowed to drink or gamble on the ranch, and the colonel would fire anyone he caught abusing a horse.

He was strictly honest and his word was good for anything in Texas that he wanted. He would keep his word regardless of the cost. Colonel Goodnight was a blunt, outspoken man but underneath his bluntness he was the kindest, most generous man I ever knew.

JAYBIRD BOB

Early the next summer, 1883, all hands were fixing to go to Mobeetie.

While we were getting ready a fellow called Jaybird Bob and another boy rode out to look after some stock down on the range.

The rest of us were told to hang around because there might be something else to do, besides going to town.

A young fellow named Jack Landrum, whose home was on the Trinity River about fifty miles below Fort Worth, Texas, rode with Rolla and me all the time.

Each of us always had a spare box of shells, a roll of jerked beef and a canvas water bottle full of water, and were ready to ride far and fast at a minute's notice.

The other boys called us "The Trinity" and we were always on the job for the J A Ranch when there was riding to be done.

In about two hours, Uncle Nick Eaton and three or four of his riders came in to go down to Mobeetie with Colonel Goodnight to a meeting of the Cattlemen's Association.

Uncle Nick and the foreman talked awhile, then came out and told the boys we could go to town whenever we wanted to, but to stay on the water wagon and be on the lookout for them when they came in.

We had all mounted and were starting out when we heard two gunshots about four seconds apart; then, after about a minute, two more shots spaced the same way.

It was the cowboy's call for help!

We all started at full speed in the direction the shots had come from.

Rolla, Jack and I got there first and met Bill, the boy who had gone out with Jaybird Bob.

"Hurry, fellows!" he called. "Some damned skunks dry gulched us out in the hills, killed Jaybird's horse, and shot him, but we drove them off. I am going back to get a buckboard to bring him in; you fellows follow the men who shot him."

We found out from him where Jaybird was and rode on.

Pretty soon Uncle Nick and his riders caught up with us. He had sent two of his boys back with Bill to get the buckboard; then he and the others followed us.

As we reached him, Jaybird, who had been lying down behind a rock, sat up and said, "They were hid up there in that pile of rocks, boys, and I heard them get their horses and ride off like the devil was after them. I thought they might come down by here but they didn't have time. I didn't get to see their faces but they will leave a trail and you boys know what to do."

A couple of the boys tied up his wounds and the rest of us rode up to the rocks that had sheltered the bushwhackers.

A HENRY RIFLE

While we were looking around I picked up a shell. It was a copper shell, forty-four and rim fire. There was only one gun that fired that shell!

"Uncle Nick," I called, "who in these parts packs a Henry rifle?"

"I know," said Nick, "and I think some of us will call on him. Now you three boys take the trail of these hombres and follow it to hell but get them. If you are not back tomorrow we will follow and see what happened."

Rolla, Jack and I started on the trail. Uncle Nick called after us, "Careful, boys, we may see you sooner than I said. It all depends on where the trail leads you."

He rode back where Jaybird was waiting for the buckboard.

Our horses were fresh and we gave them their heads

The trail was easy to follow, we were all good trackers, and so we covered the ground rapidly.

We pushed on until it got too dark to see the trail, then Jack and I gave our reins to Rolla and while we followed the trail on foot he led the ponies.

About nine o'clock that night we came to a spring. After watering our ponies and filling our water bottles we pulled off our boots and washed our feet.

Then we struck out on the trail again.

About two o'clock in the morning we came to another spring and found where the men we were trailing had watered their horses and ridden on.

The signs were fresh and we went on more carefully now with Rolla and the horses well to the rear.

The moon went down and, afraid of losing the trail, we were about to stop until daylight when we saw the light of a lamp in the window of a cabin a short distance away.

Tying our ponies, we crept forward to investigate.

THE CABIN

Just below us there was a creek. On the further bank, past a large water hole in the creek, was a small house.

Some men were moving about in the lamplight. By this time it was light enough to see our way around. We looked things over and made our plans.

The cabin was about fifty yards from the creek on a little grassy knoll.

Back of it was the horse corral and in the lot were four tired horses standing with their heads down, resting.

So then we were sure their riders were our bushwhackers.

After a while the men put out the light and went to bed.

We went back to our horses and tied them where they could get grass and water and got our water bottles, spare shells and some jerky.

In the horse lot there was a log about two feet thick, with holes chopped in it and filled with salt, to make a salt lick. It also made a pretty good shelter for a man to hide behind.

The door of the cabin faced the creek about fifty yards away, and there was a path where they carried up the water.

There was a window in each side of the cabin and a fireplace at the back.

Rolla went up the creek until he got in front of the window where he found a washout that gave him an ideal shelter. There was high grass all around the washout and the window faced the corral.

Jack laid down behind the lick log and waited, chewing on a piece of jerky.

I laid under the creek bank directly in front of the door. The bank was about three feet high, covered with grass, and made a perfect place for concealment.

After we all learned where the others were stationed, we ate jerky and drank water and waited for the men in the house to show up.

Jack had let the bars down so their horses could get out, thinking that might bring the men out to put the horses back into the corral.

The bushwhackers must have been very tired, for it was an hour after sunrise before there was any sign of life from the cabin. Then a small wisp of smoke came out of the chimney and we all got ready for action.

FRONTIER JUSTICE

Presently the door opened and a man came out.

He had a wooden bucket hanging in the crook of his right arm and in the crook of his left arm was a Henry rifle! He had his right hand on the breech of the gun as he stepped out and looked around.

He looked back at the trail he had come in on, the night before.

Then came what sounded like just one report. The man's knees buckled and he went down on his face, in the dust of the path to the spring, with three bullets, from three Winchesters, through him.

We put a few more shots into the door and each window and went on eating jerky waiting for another shot.

There was no movement in the house until about noon.

Then Rolla saw the rawhide curtains over the window move to one side.

He promptly put three or four shots through the window and Jack and I fired five or six shots apiece.

The smoke from our guns — this was before the days of smoke-less powder — gave our positions away, so the outlaws fired at our smoke.

But they hit nothing.

There was a long silence.

One of the men called out three or four times but we didn't answer.

Pretty soon the men started shooting through the cracks in the house and we swapped smoke with them for a few minutes, then let them do all the firing, thinking they might get careless and expose themselves. But they never did.

HELP ARRIVES

About the middle of the afternoon a bunch of horsemen came over the hill and we were worried until we saw it was Uncle Nick Eaton and a bunch of the J A cowboys.

We fired several shots to show them where we were hiding and they sized up the way things were going.

Nick stopped his men out of range of gunshot, divided them up and came on in.

Two of Nick's men came to each of us boys, and Nick and the rest of his men circled around the house and took positions in the timber.

While the men in the house were shooting at us, Nick's men piled a lot of brush and logs at the back of the house and set it on fire.

The smoke blew out in front and we all got ready for the break.

The men in the house called and Nick answered.

They wanted to know what terms he would give them, if they would give up.

211

"The same terms you gave our men!" yelled Nick.

"You can have your choice. Stay in there and roast like rats, or come out shooting and we will shoot you like the dogs you are. Or come out with your hands up and we will hang you to that Cottonwood tree."

They came out shooting, but not a man got away.

We camped that night at the water hole and Nick's men stood guard.

The next morning we started back to the ranch. When we arrived Jaybird Bob had died.

Uncle Charlie Goodnight had sent to Mobeetie for a real coffin and a preacher.

We dug Jaybird's grave at the edge of the rim rock by three tall trees and laid him where he could look out for miles over the finest range in the world: big pools of clear water, tall grass and herds of cattle, horses and buffalo grazing in all directions.

There was no one to crowd him, for there was not another grave within twenty-five miles of him.

There he sleeps alone with his gun on his breast and his saddle in the grave with him.

Peace to his clay!

He lived and died like a man; who wants more than that?

We never knew Jaybird Bob's real name, but he is on the roll by the name his friends all called him. Jaybird Bob!

Names don't matter.

He will be remembered by the men who avenged him.

16 THE FAMOUS GOODNIGHT BLUFF

THERE was a Cattlemen's Convention at Mobectie, Texas, and Colonel Charles Goodnight and Uncle Nick Eaton were up there for two days.

When they came back they got all hands together and told them to clean their thirty- thirties, wrap them in a blanket with two boxes of shells and put them into the chuck wagon, get their best ponies and get ready to ride to town.

We didn't know what was going on and for that matter didn't care.

We rode along with the chuck wagon and camped on the outskirts of Mobeetie.

We were a disappointed bunch of cowboys, though, when we got strict orders to stay in camp.

But when we saw Nick Eaton's chuck wagon and riders, and outfits from some of the other ranches, come in and camp near us we began to wonder what was up.

After a while Colonel Goodnight's foreman, a man named Pennington, told us to come on — so we got on our ponies and started for town.

We were joined by boys from the other outfits, and we made a hard-boiled bunch of riders.

The foreman of each outfit took his riders up to the place where the cattlemen were holding their meeting. We left our horses at the hitch rack, filed into the room, lined up against the wall and listened.

Colonel Goodnight was talking and he said something like this: "We have enough evidence against them to hang every damn one of them and that

213

is what is going to happen right away. I have eighteen good riders, every one a fighting man. Every one has a thirty-thirty, besides his belt guns, and we have lost all the cattle we are going to lose. Now we will clear the room and not let anyone in that is not a cowpuncher. Each foreman must vouch for all his men. We will fix up our plans and give the boys the names of the men we want and they can bring them in. Then we will hold court and give them justice. Now, all you owners keep your scats; and everybody else must go. A foreman will be at each door to see that everyone who comes in belongs in. This is a cattlemen's meeting for the purpose of stopping cow thieves; no one but cattlemen and their hands will be allowed. Pennington, who is my fore-man, will vouch for the men he has with him. Nick Eaton, here, and his boys are ready. You other men are as ready as you ever will be so let's clear out all but the cattlemen and get to work. Clear the room, boys."

The boys got busy and started to clear the room.

There were a lot of town loafers and shady characters, who wanted to stay and hear what was coming off, but they were all put out and two guards were stationed at each door and window.

The foremen stood at the doors and let in only their own men.

After they were all settled down, Nick Eaton and Deaf Smith, another big cattle owner, went out and the others just sat around and waited for them to come back.

When they did come back they were laughing; they told the other cattlemen their plan was working and they all laughed.

Then Colonel Goodnight said, "Pennington, take the boys down and line them up against the wall in the saloon and let them stand there awhile and wait for orders. Now, they will try to get you to drink; but I don't want any damn one of you to take a drink of any kind, so tell them you haven't got time now but you will later. Now don't talk to anyone, just go in and line up with your backs against the wall and stand there until we send for you."

It was a very quiet town just then. There were over fifty armed cowboys in the different groups and they went into every saloon and dance hall in town and nobody wanted to start any trouble with them as they stood silently waiting for orders.

They wondered what the orders would be and there were a good many others in the town that would have liked to know.

In that brief time there were eighteen men who left town and went to the hills to camp until they could learn how things were going to turn out.

After we had stood there for about half an hour the foreman came in and said, "Come on, boys, they are going to wait until morning and make a clean sweep of the whole shebang. Let's get back to camp."

We all filed out and went to the chuck wagon where the cook had supper ready and the foreman said, "Stay in camp, boys; don't anyone go to town tonight. We have them on the run and in the morning we will finish up and h'ist a few drinks and go back home."

Pennington went over and joined the bosses and they all rode into town and went around asking for certain men who they knew had left town.

Then, a little later, when they saw a man ride out of town, they knew he was taking word to the suspects who had left for the hills earlier in the day, so they let him go — for that was part of the game.

The next morning Pennington told Rolla, Jack and me to get our rifles and go with him and the others.

When we reached the first saloon we saw the other foremen, with small squads of cowboys, going into the other saloons and dance halls and wondered what it meant.

Pennington went up to the barkeeper and asked for a man by name. The barkeeper said the man had not been in that morning and he guessed he was down at his boarding place.

Pennington answered that we had just come from there and he was not there. Then he turned to us and said, "Come on, boys, we will find him if we have to go all over hell with a fine-tooth comb."

We turned and walked out and went over to where the boys from the other outfits had gathered.

Pretty soon we saw another horseman ride out of town, in the direction of the hills, hell bent for leather.

We stood around a little while longer; then the foreman said, "All right, boys, go wet your whistle but don't take too much. If anyone wants to know what we are going to do, tell him you don't know but that you have orders to wait and then maybe take a ride in the hills. Now, don't drink too much and don't let any man kick you into a fight."

The boys scattered and the foremen and the ranchers had a celebration of their own laughing over the trick they had played.

Of the eighteen men that left town that night only three ever came back. They were very careful for a long time not to lay a rope on a calf and when they did they were promptly hung by the Vigilantes.

Late the next morning the different outfits started for home.

They had broken the cow-stealing ring without firing a single shot, and it stayed that way for a long time.

They still laugh, down there in Texas, about Colonel Goodnight's bluff.

WHOOPING IT UP, IN TOWN

After the spring roundup, 1884, Colonel Goodnight and the J A outfit took a herd up the trail to Kansas, where the colonel sold them.

The cattle were shipped from Caldwell, Kansas, to Kansas City and the colonel went along with them to Kansas City.

We made camp at the edge of town where we were to wait until the colonel came back.

It was just at the beginning of the depression of the middle '80's, but money was getting tight and so was credit for the cattlemen.

Talk among the cowhands was that the Colonel had gone to Kansas City to look into the situation.

After the cattle were shipped the boys all got paid and went into Caldwell to have some fun.

Rolla and I did not drink but we went along to see the sights and there sure were plenty of them.

The town was full of railroaders, cowboys, freighters and traders, buffalo hunters, gamblers and loafers of all kinds.

The dance halls and saloons were running wide open.

We took turns going to town; part of the boys had to stay in camp and take care of the remuda, that's the saddle horses, and the stuff in camp.

When the bunch got back from town they watched the things and let the boys who had stayed at camp go in and look around.

Rolla and I were watching the dancers one night when a couple of pretty girls came up and asked us to dance.

It was the old-fashioned square dance and we were having lots of fun.

There were about thirty-five railroaders in the room and two of them had partners in the same set. They were drinking heavily and could hardly stand on their feet.

Pretty soon the dancers got all tangled up and the floor manager was trying to straighten them out.

One of the drunks came over and grabbed my girl and started back to his set with her.

The girl broke away from him and slapped his face and just as I came up he struck at her with his fist. I caught his arm and struck him right under the ear, knocking him out cold.

There was a roar from the railroaders on the sidelines and they all started for the dance floor.

Rolla and I backed against the wall and drew our guns. Telling the girls to get into the other room, we waited for the mob to come on.

The other boys from our outfit were at the bar watching. They all drew their guns and one of them shot the light out while he backed away toward the door.

Our ponies were tied just outside.

There were all kinds and sizes of guns working at the same time, from thirty-twos to forty-fives — and the gamblers were shooting their derringers, short-barreled pocket pistols of large caliber.

The air was filled with yells, screams and oaths.

The forty-fives of the cowboys were belching fire clear across the room as we scrambled for the door.

Outside, finding that we were all there, we got on our ponies and, shooting in the air a few times as we rode past the door, we headed for camp.

The foreman was sitting on the wagon tongue and was sure surprised to see us ride in so early, all sober.

"What the hell is the matter with you fellows?" he asked. "Have they run out of whisky and shipped all the girls out? What's the reason for your getting in this time of night?"

"We joined the W.C.T.U.," Charlie Siringo replied.

One of the boys who had stayed in camp said, "Hey, boys, it's not late; let's go to town and start in where they left off."

"Well, go ahead, fellows," said Charlie, "but I don't think the J A cowboys would be very welcome at the dance hall we just left."

He gave them a rough idea of the fight and when he had finished, the foreman saddled up his pony and rode into town to see what had really happened.

The boys all waited for him to come back until after midnight. Then they went to bed and Rolla, Jack Landrum and I started out to look for the foreman.

We met him not far from camp, riding along sampling the contents of a jug that hung from his saddle horn.

"It's all right, boys!" he called to us. "I talked to the manager of the dance hall and he said it was all the fault of those drunken railroaders. He said you boys just finished up what he started to do. He made the railroaders pay the damages, and just so there would be no hard feelings he gave me this jug of good whisky."

219

The next day the foreman took the wagon to town and had it loaded for the trip home.

Colonel Goodnight got back from Kansas City that day, so the next morning we pulled out for the J A.

When we arrived at the ranch we found Quanah Parker, with a band of Indian warriors and their womenfolk, camped in the lower end of the canyon.

Quanah Parker was Chief of the Comanche Indians. His mother, Cynthia Ann Parker, was a white woman. She had been captured as a child and raised by the Comanche Indians. When she was grown she had married a Comanche warrior, so Quanah, their son, was only half Indian.

Colonel Goodnight and Quanah Parker were firm friends and they were glad to see each other.

The colonel drove some beeves down to the Indian camp and there was feasting and dancing among the warriors and their squaws. And the colonel knew his cattle were safe from marauding Comanches for a long time.

HEREFORDS

Colonel Charles Goodnight was always interested in the progress of the cattle business. He was a real old-time cattle king and he was always trying to improve his breeds.

He was a great leader and had far-sighted vision.

He was one of the cattlemen who organized the Panhandle Stock Association in the early '80's to protect themselves against the spreading of Texas fever by infected herds passing over their ranges.

The colonel tried to bring the Hereford cattle into Texas but they died with the Texas fever almost as soon as he got them there.

220

The Texas longhorns were immune to the disease and the colonel knew there was a way to immunize the Herefords, too, if he could only find it.

He tried everything he heard about but the Herefords just kept on dying.

One day Rolla and I were out on the range sitting on the grass watching the cattle. We got to talking about the Herefords and the Texas fever.

Rolla said that he had been thinking about it and he believed if the young Hereford calf was taken away from its mother as soon as it was born and not allowed to suck but given to a Texas cow that was immune to the fever, the calf might become immune to the disease.

His idea sounded sort of reasonable and I urged Rolla to go to his Uncle Charlie and talk to him about it, so when we went back to the ranch Rolla went to the colonel and told him what he had been thinking.

The colonel thought it might work, too, so he tried it.

We used to take the Hereford calf as soon as we found it, and give it to a native cow. We would milk the native cow's milk all over the calf, then she would mother it.

It was slow but it worked and it was one of the many things that helped the Hereford cattle to live in Texas.

Bulls were imported but they still died of the fever.

It was not until a generation or two of Herefords were raised in Texas that they were immune to the Texas fever.

Later there were better ways, but that was one of the first things that was tried with any success.

That was the beginning of the Hereford cattle in Texas.

THE PARSON

In the fall, 1884, Colonel Goodnight, Nick Eaton and Deaf Smith gathered up a bunch of cattle in the central part of Texas and drove them through to Caldwell, Kansas, to be shipped east.

A nice-looking boy came into our camp just before we started the drive and wanted to ride through to Kansas with us.

The boss gave him a job as horse wrangler. He was a good, clean-looking boy and had a beautiful singing voice.

He was rather small but well put together and had a quiet retiring disposition. He never drank, used tobacco or swore and was always ready to help anybody.

For his good qualities we called him Parson.

Whenever the boys got rough, talking or acting tough, the Parson always had to go look after his horses.

He never carried a gun and showed good breeding and good sense in every move he made.

The Parson helped drive clear through to Caldwell, Kansas.

When we got to Bluff Creek, where we camped at the end of the drive, the Parson quit and the boss paid him off.

He shook hands with all of us and went to town when the wagon went in for supplies.

The next day Rolla and I were saddling up to go out on the afternoon watch when Rolla let out a whoop and said, "Hold me down, buddy, look what's coming!"

I looked and saw a lady riding the trail toward camp. She had on a long black riding habit with a pink silk waist and a big black hat with a long curly ostrich plume around the crown and was riding sidesaddle.

She rode up alongside of us and said, "Hello, fellows, where you going?"

I looked at her a minute and then I said, "I don't know, I guess I'm going crazy, I believe I've seen you before."

She laughed, "Why, Frank, don't you know Parson?"

Rolla took off his hat and said, "Well, I'll be damned! Oh, excuse me, Parson, for swearing."

Some of the other boys gathered round and we all apologized for some of the language we had used on the trail.

The Parson explained to us she had been obliged to get from Texas to Topeka, Kansas, and since there was no railroad across the Indian Territory, she had decided to join up with us on our drive, letting on all the time that she was a boy.

Now that we had reached the railroad at Caldwell, she could go on to Topeka by train. But she said she just couldn't leave without telling us all good-by.

THE SCHOOLTEACHER

After we got back home to the J A ranch, Colonel

Goodnight had us drive a herd of about forty-five hundred head of cattle to another range.

223

We were west of Fort Worth, Texas, and had five brands of cattle in the herd, all Texas longhorns, and a few extra longhorns.

One day we passed a schoolhouse. In those days you had a fence wherever you didn't want the cattle to get in, so the schoolhouse was fenced in.

The schoolteacher and all the children were out in the yard watching the cattle go by. The teacher was small and young and just as pretty as she could be. By gosh, she was a beauty!

We rode within about twenty steps of the schoolhouse.

Rolla was riding just ahead of me in the swing and I was on the flank. When we got up to the schoolhouse I hollered at Rolla, "Oh Rolla, let's stop off right here and finish our education."

Rolla hollered back, "We'll draw our money tonight and come back."

Then we rode on.

Up at Enid, Oklahoma, in 1945, Rolla and I had been helping a girl named Betty Jo Glover with some historical facts for a historical-event contest in which she won first prize.

We were there when the prize was awarded and after the ceremony was over Betty Jo said, "Let's go over and visit Grandma. She is an old Texas schoolteacher and I know she would like to meet you men. Her name is Grandma Swindler."

So we went over to meet Grandma Swindler — Betty Jo, her mother and father and Rolla and I.

The old lady's hair was just as white as milk, long and wavy and shiny as silk. She wasn't any bigger than a prairie dog but just as spry as a three-year-old.

224

By George, she was active! She could still see pretty good too.

Mr. Glover introduced us as a couple of old Texas cowhands.

She shook hands with us and said, "It's good to meet some of the old boys from Texas. I used to know lots of Texas cowhands. When I was young I used to teach school out west of Fort Worth.

One day there was a big herd of Texas cattle going by the schoolhouse and the children wouldn't study anyway so I let them all out in the yard to look at the cattle. The herd had pretty near got past the school when one of the fellows called out to a fellow up ahead of him, 'Let's stop here and finish our education.' The other one answered, 'Wait till we draw our money and we'll come back,' but they never did."

I looked at Rolla and laughed. "Oh yes, they did," I said, "We're here to finish up!"

BUCKSKIN PETE'S FIGHT WITH THE INDIANS

Rolla and I were still riding, helping drive a bunch of cattle up the Chisholm Trail. There were two water holes close together; we had made one by noon and could make the other by night but there was a herd ahead of us and we didn't know what they were going to do.

As I have said, in driving a herd of cattle the cowboys out in front are called the "pointers"; the ones you see riding along the side of the herd are the "swing," and the cowboys behind the herd looking after the stragglers are the "drag."

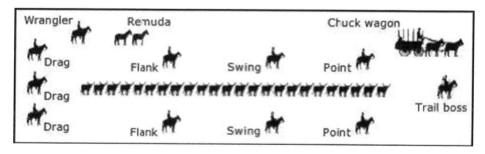

225

Buckskin Pete was working on the drag; but he was always rarin' to go and he had a good horse, so the boss sent him up to see about the herd ahead.

Pete had only been gone a little while when we heard gunshots up ahead.

The boss was in the point; he stopped the cattle and everybody went except two drags, the horse wrangler and the cook.

We went over a rise all strung out, the fastest horse in the lead, and riding hell for leather.

Pretty soon we saw Pete's horse, dead, right in the trail, and out to one side a cloud of smoke hanging over a buffalo wallow. The wallow was full of rosinweeds with Pete in the middle of them building up a big smoke from his gun.

Riding in a circle around the buffalo wallow were fifteen or twenty Indians. Pete had killed two or three of their horses and the dismounted Indians were on the slope of the hill right where we went over.

They had taken a position where they could watch for help to come to Pete, but they had thought he belonged to the herd up ahead and that help would come from that direction. They jumped up when they saw us . . . but they didn't go any place.

One Indian was between us and Pete; he looked back at us over his shoulder and took out straight across the buffalo wallow where Pete was, but he got too close — to Pete.

I had emptied my rifle and leaned forward to get my guns when my horse got a bullet right between the eyes; it came out in back of his neck and glanced off my saddle horn; I went off him and landed on my head.

Just as I got my gun I saw three Indians coming back to get my scalp, shooting as they came.

226

I staggered back to my horse and got behind him to use him for breastworks; my eyes were kind of blurred and I couldn't see very well, but they were coming right in after me; I looked back and there was Buckskin Pete. I looked again at the Indians but Pete had just kept shooting and there weren't any Indians there. I didn't even get a shot.

Altogether there was only one Indian left; he was making for one of the boys we called Long Tom.

Long Tom had emptied his gun and before he could load it the Indian would have had his scalp, but Tom was a good man with a rope — and that was quicker, so he threw his lariat and roped the redskin and you should have seen that Indian bounce.

INDIAN STRTEGY

We were driving a mixed herd for five different owners; Jim Flood was trail boss and Jim Connelly was one of the owners.

Charlie Nida, Lee Keyes, Buckskin Pete and a half dozen other boys were in Connelly's string and he rode as a hand.

The trail crossed the North Canadian River east of where El Reno, Oklahoma, now stands.

Old Fort Reno, a cavalry garrison, was west of there just across the Canadian River from the Darlington Agency, which was on the north bank of the North Canadian River. But we had some more trouble with Indians and crossed the river farther east and missed the Darlington Agency and Fort Reno by several miles.

A band of Indians were camped there by the trail and as a bunch of us came up with the herd the Indians came down to meet us saying they wanted to buy some cattle.

When the Indians bought the cattle they would pick them out of the herd and we always got a good price.

They told us they were going to have a powwow and they would charge us one steer for going through their camp and then buy forty head.

They paid the boss one hundred and sixty dollars and were going to pay the balance when they got the steers. They said they would come that afternoon and get them.

THE BOY IN THE ROCK PILE

There was a big pile of rocks around a spring off at the side of the trail and we soon learned that the Indians had a prisoner in the rock pile.

We asked one of them about it and he told us the fellow in the rock pile was a boy about fifteen or sixteen years old. He was driving a bunch of ponies, about a hundred, from Texas up to Kansas and he was by himself, playing a lone hand.

When the boy came up the trail to the place where the Indians were camped the headman had gone out and told him he would have to pay for going through their camp.

The boy said he would not pay because it was a free trail and he was going through. He was so brave the Indians told him he could go through for one pony. He told them to go to hell!

The Indian took down his rope and roped one of the boy's ponies and started to lead it off.

The boy fired one shot and the Indian toppled off his pony — dead.

Other Indians were coming.

The boy saw the pile of rocks around the spring and he made for it with his packhorse. He threw his packhorse loose and turned his saddle horse out where he could get grass and water. He was well supplied with ammunition and grub and fixed to stand quite a fight.

The Indians tried to rush him at first but they soon found that was going to be too costly, so they just surrounded him and thought they would starve him out.

About that time we came up the trail.

About two o'clock that afternoon a big bunch of Indians rode up on a hill and made the peace sign.

The boss answered and put two of us boys about forty yards apart and as the Indians rode down between us we looked them over to see if they had any shooting irons.

While the Indian Chief was down talking to our boss the rest of them divided up and went to each of us cowboys.

There were about nine Indian riders on our side, three came up to me, one on each side and one right in front of my pony. They were begging for tobacco. I didn't have any tobacco and told them so, but they didn't budge.

One old buck was sitting out in front of us.

He didn't go in to look at the cattle and he wasn't begging tobacco. He didn't seem to have any part in the whole thing, he just sat there.

Then all at once he threw back his head and gave a loud war whoop. The three Indians that were standing beside me closed in.

The one in front grabbed my horse while the ones at each side took my gun and one pushed me while the other pulled — and before I knew what was happening they had me on the ground and disarmed. I looked around and all the other boys were in the same predicament; they took the whole bunch of us without firing a single shot.

At that time about a hundred Indians came riding in and drove our cattle out west of the trail a ways; they loaded us in our own chuck wagon and took us down to their camp, about a half-mile west of the rock pile.

They told us about the fellow in the rock pile and explained that they would give us back our cattle and let us go on, after they had killed him, but they couldn't let us go through for fear we would tell the soldiers at Fort Reno and they would come and get him out.

The Indians stretched some lariats around our chuck wagon and made a corral. They told us to stay inside and we would not get hurt, but if we got outside that rope they would shoot us.

They left about twenty braves to guard us and the rest went back to the camp.

That night one of the boys crawled out and got a horse and struck out for Fort Reno.

The Indians didn't find it out until the next morning. When we went to eat breakfast they counted us. One brave came in and asked where the other man was. We told him we thought the men were all there and we looked around real innocent-like. But it didn't work; the Indians got mad and that night they tied us up; they tied our feet together and tied our hands behind our backs.

The Indians had been sending out signals with signal fires and other Indians were coming in all the time in answer to them.

Hundreds of them, mostly Cheyennes, came from all directions.

They made three or four runs down on the rock pile and lost some Indians every time.

They had killed the boy's saddle horse but the boy was still there and every time an Indian got too close he let him have it — right between the eyes.

230

THE CAVALRY

About noon on the third day we saw a cloud of dust rising way up on the trail to the north of us and it was not long before we could see the cavalry coming.

There were half a dozen soldiers in the lead, about one hundred and fifty yards ahead of the main column, and some out on each side about one hundred yards from the main column.

Way behind we could see the white wagon sheets of the ambulances and supply wagons. There were four mules to each wagon and guards all around.

The cavalry uniform was blue, with a yellow stripe down the trouser leg, a blue blouse trimmed with yellow and brass buttons, black boots and a regulation cavalry hat.

The horses were beautiful, mostly bays but some chestnuts and sorrels, and a few blacks, but no paints or other fancy horses.

A cavalry horse weighed somewhere around eleven hundred pounds while a cow pony weighed only about nine hundred.

When the lead soldiers got within about three to four hundred yards of them the Indians started shooting.

The soldiers stopped then and the main column came on up and formed two columns with about four feet between.

The Indians were bunching up on the creek toward the rock pile.

A Medicine Man was leading the Indians to attack.

He had on a war bonnet and was telling them the white man's bullets couldn't kill an Indian with a war bonnet on.

He was going through all sorts of contortions while he told them he was making the white man's gunpowder turn to dirt so it would not kill the Indians.

An officer with a straight sword, not a cavalry saber, in his hand came riding down the line of soldiers. He stopped in front of one of them and pointed with his sword to the Medicine Man. The soldier raised his carbine and sighted, for just a second, then fired; and the Medicine Man pitched headfirst off his pony, war bonnet and all, with a bullet clear through him.

The soldiers started their horses. They rode at a slow trot at first, then a faster trot, then a run. When they got within about fifty yards of the Indians they raised their guns and fired.

The Indians had been shooting at them all the time but the soldiers hadn't fired a shot until then.

The smoke from the guns covered the line of soldiers but when they came out of that smoke and dust every man had his saber in his hand and was riding like the wind.

We were on a little rise southwest of them and the sun was shining right on them. We could see the sabers glitter in the sun and hear the rattle of them against the Indians' guns.

They were making a saber charge.

When a cavalry horse makes a charge he goes in with his nose and tail straight out and his ears back.

He goes straight ahead and nothing stops him unless he is killed. If another horse gets in his way he just runs over him.

An Indian in the back broke and ran, then two or three, then fifteen or twenty.

After a few minutes of fighting they all broke and ran.

Our guards had run with the rest of the Indians and I rolled over to Buckskin Pete and he untied my hands with his teeth; then I untied him. (We had been in the sun all day, and when I had complained about the heat Pete had said, "Better enjoy this; if them soldiers don't get here we will be in a damned sight hotter place than this!")

In a short time we were all free and went down where the fighting had been.

The ambulances had come in and they were picking up the wounded men; there were quite a few dead horses.

The soldiers came back after a while with what was left of the Indians, but most of them got away.

There must have been around three hundred soldiers and two or three times that many Indians.

The poor devil in the rock pile had come out and gone down to the creek.

He was drinking water and washing his face. His tongue was so thick he couldn't swear. There was a little spring in the rock pile but it had dried up and he had been without water all day.

We found our horses and fighting irons and the mules we had hooked to the chuck wagon, but the cattle were scattered all over, some of them clear back to Big Red.

It took us two days to get them rounded up and on our way again — but we felt lucky to be alive.

BACK TO THE TERRITORY

The next spring, 1885, when roundup time was over, Rolla and I left the J A and started back to the Indian Territory.

First we went to Arkansas City to see Captain Knipe and he put us both to work for the Cattlemen's Association.

Rolla went down to the K K Ranch and Captain Knipe sent me down to Elgin, Kansas, to catch some cattle thieves.

I was back on my old job again.

17 INDIAN TERRITORY

ELGIN, KANSAS

ELGIN, Kansas, was a little town on the state line two or three miles north of the Osage Nation, Indian Territory.

My job was to catch some cattle thieves who had been butchering stolen cattle and selling them to the markets in Elgin.

The thieves would drive down into the Nation, kill a beef, load it into their wagon and be gone in an hour.

They could be arrested on suspicion but there was no way to identify a skinned and dressed beef, and you had to have proof for conviction, which was hard to get.

There were plenty of crooks who would swear they had sold the animal to the rustlers and then get a rake-off for their perjured testimony.

The law officer would get the horselaugh and, also, he would be a marked man. Soon he would be found dead; and the thieves would all "wonder how it happened," and wink — and go after another load of beef.

I knew all this and intended to make sure I had the evidence to convict the lawbreakers when I got them.

First I found out who was selling the stolen beef.

Then I watched when the meat ran low to find out who the man was that supplied the market. I shadowed him.

But, do all I knew how to do, the rustlers still came in with the meat and I had only hard riding for my trouble; but I hung on, hoping for better luck next time.

One evening I was in Tom Leahey's store playing checkers with one of the men who sold the stolen beef.

Just as we were finishing a game, his partner came in and nodded to him. The fellow got up and said, "Well, I guess that's enough for one night. I'm going home and go to bed."

"Me, too," I said and got up and went out and hid where I could watch them when they came out of the store.

Their market was next door to Leahey's and pretty soon I saw them come out and go to their barn. They harnessed up their team and hitched it to a spring wagon, threw in their butchering tools and drove out of town on the east road.

I saddled my pony and was after them in a few minutes.

I followed them to where the roads forked and found they had turned off and gone down into the Osage Nation. I followed the road, looking for their tracks to turn off, but didn't see any place where they had turned.

I rode for hours and never saw them again.

Finally I gave up and camped in the hills and the next morning I rode back and found where they had turned into a rocky draw and I had ridden on without seeing the place.

THE CARPENTER BRAND

Taking their trail I soon came to the place where they had killed their beef and after trailing around I found the hide and part of the entrails in a washout, covered with rocks.

236

The wolves had already dug through the rocks and eaten the entrails, and had dragged the hide part way out from under the rocks.

I looked at the brand and found that the animal had belonged to the Carpenter Ranch.

I knew Mr. Carpenter, so I rode down to his ranch and asked him if he had sold any cattle to be butchered.

He called his foreman and asked him if any cattle had been sold from the ranch and the foreman said no, there had not been.

I told them about finding the hide and entrails of a beef and the foreman rode out with me to the place where I had found them. He looked at the hide and saw the Carpenter brand and he knew it was their cow.

We looked for the wagon tracks and trailed them back to the road. The foreman rode on in to Elgin with me and we saw that beef in the market, on the block, ready for sale.

There wasn't anything we could do about it then, so we went down to Leahey's store and had a lunch.

After that we went to my room and made war medicine and when we had our plans made the foreman returned to the ranch and I went back to watching my men.

THEY NEED BEEF!

Soon the meat was getting low in the market again, and I was keeping a close watch on the men for I knew they would be going out for more beef any night.

This time I was determined I'd catch them.

I sent word to Carpenter's foreman and told my landlady I was going on a trip.

I met the foreman in the hills and we camped and kept watch on all the roads.

We had been there for three days when we saw one of the cowboys from the Carpenter ranch drive a bunch of cattle out in the bottoms and leave them there; then he rode on into town.

Late that afternoon we saw three men in a spring wagon coming down the road.

We rode up to the end of the draw where I had found the cowhide and waited. Sure enough, the third man was the cowboy from the Carpenter ranch.

We waited until they had shot the cattle and were skinning them; then we had the proof we needed.

The foreman yelled, "Hands up!" and they looked into the muzzles of three six-guns; I always wore two.

The two thieves had only their skinning knives and they gave up but the cowboy drew his gun and the foreman drilled him — center.

We made the thieves load the two beeves and the dead cowboy into the spring wagon and we drove them to town.

We turned our prisoners over to the sheriff along with the stolen cows and the dead cowboy. The sheriff locked up the two thieves and that was the first time I ever saw a cattle thief held for trial; justice had always been meted out right on the spot — but times were changing.

The two thieves had the best lawyers in the country. They claimed they were working for the dead cowboy and thought he had authority to sell the cattle.

The trial was put off and finally they were released on bond and went to selling beef again.

I was still on the job for the Cattlemen's Association and had to stay until the case was settled.

JUSTICE

One night when a bunch of us were down at Leahey's store a railroad detective was doing some sleight-of-hand tricks for the amusement of the boys. He was making a coin disappear and one of the cattle thieves bet him ten dollars he knew where the coin was. But when he discovered the coin wasn't where he thought it was, he got mad.

He motioned to his buddy, and the two of them got up and went outside.

Old Bill, the detective, looked after them and grinned.

A few minutes later he got up to leave. I saw he had drawn his gun and was going out with it in his hand. As he told me later, he flattened himself against the wall until he came to the corner of the building.

On the other side, at the corner, he saw the two men waiting.

They opened fire.

But Bill was ready for them. When the shooting was over he had a bullet in his left arm but one of the cattle thieves was dead and the other was dying with two bullets through his body.

My job was finished.

MISSION CREEK

Joe Herod down on Mission Creek had sent word that he was losing a large number of calves and yearlings and Captain Knipe had told me when I got through at Elgin to go down there and see what I could do about it.

So after Bill got the cattle thieves at Elgin I started getting ready to go down to investigate.

I was all ready to leave when Joe's son Ike and three of the ranch hands came into town and began to celebrate. They asked me to wait and ride down with them, so I tied my pony and waited, and in about two hours we started out. Ike and each of the three cowboys had a gallon jug of whisky in a tow sack tied on the back of his saddle and there was a pint apiece in the saddle pockets, and all they could carry besides.

They rode out of town shooting and yelling like the devil on a tear.

JOE HEROD

Joe Herod was a Frenchman who had married an Osage Indian woman and taken a large block of land. He had a fair-sized herd of cattle.

Joe liked his whisky and had sent the boys to town after some, so when we got to the ranch he was waiting for them.

He liked company in his drinking so he had invited in three of the neighbors. They were all dry as powder horns and the first jug hardly lasted until it got around.

Joe gave orders that all the boys were to turn over their guns to me to keep until the party was over.

So I took them out to the barn, wrapped them in a saddle blanket and hid them in the manger, under the hay where the horses were eating. Then I filled the manger full of hay.

When I got back to the house the boys had emptied all of the pint bottles and had started on the second jug.

Joe told them that I would stand guard while he took one jug out and hid it so they would have it to sober up on in the morning.

When Joe came back two of the boys had gone to sleep so we put them on some blankets and Joe and I started to sing. Joe sang in French and I sang in English; two of the other boys joined in and sang in Osage; but we were all singing the same songs.

One of the boys had an old drum and the rest of us were dancing the old Indian stomp dance. Every time they sat down to rest they all took a drink.

About midnight the whisky supply began running low and Ike accused his father of hiding more than one jug.

They quarreled.

Finally Ike went into the kitchen and came back with a big butcher knife. He started for his old man and Joe ran around the house with Ike after him.

After a few times around, Ike was gaining on his father, so one of the boys threw a saddle out in front of Ike. That slowed him down for a couple of rounds, then Joe looked over his shoulder and saw him gaining again. He yelled out, "Ikey, Ikey, you no-good Indian. Don't you know your own lovin' father?" Then he tore out again

While they were making the circle around the house I got my lariat and as Ike came by I roped him.

A couple of the boys hogtied him with a pigging string and gave him another drink and he passed out.

We tied him to a porch post and put a blanket over him.

Joe sat on the edge of the porch and cursed him as soon as he could get enough wind.

Finally Joe said, "By God, boys, he would have got me in a few more rounds, I was nearly done for and he was running better all the time. I didn't know he could run so fast.

I'm going to train him and run him against John Swanick and Jasper Exendine."

After resting a while he got the jug and when he turned loose of it he was ready to be put to bed.

The rest of us rolled into our blankets and the next thing we knew it was about ten o'clock in the morning and Ike was yelling for someone to untie him.

We all got up and Joe went out to hunt for the jug he had hid the night before. He was pretty well snooted when he hid it, and had now forgotten where it was; but he finally found it and they all took a drink while Alf Brown and I started breakfast.

MY FIRST DRINK

While we were eating breakfast Joe asked, "Say, Frank, how come you didn't drink last night?"

"Well," I said, "if I had, I might not have caught Ike on that first throw and he would have been cutting steaks off you before he got around the house again. And if I hadn't got a good heeler on him the boys couldn't have held him."

"That's right," said one of the boys, "if Frank had been drinking no telling what might have happened. But now there is just a little left in the jug and we think you ought to take a drink, Frank, so we will know you don't think you are too good to drink with us."

Joe Herod joined in so I said, "Well, fellows, if that is the way you feel about it, here goes for my first drink."

I turned up the jug and took a swallow of the whisky and nearly choked to death on it.

They all laughed and then each one showed me how it was done. Joe said, "Well, my boy, now I see why your nerves never bother you when you get in a fight and I don't blame you. In your business you have to have steady nerves and good eyes to make a living job out of it. But me, I will just go on drinking and hire my fighting done."

He turned up the jug again. Then he turned to me and said, "Frank, did you come down to look after my calf crop for me?"

I told him that I did, and they all offered to help in any way they could.

Then Joe said, "There isn't enough whisky left to make us quarrelsome, so while the other boys wash the dishes and clean the house, Frank, you go get our guns."

I went back to the barn and got their guns.

"I am damned glad you had these hid," said Ike as he strapped his belt guns on. "Father, I want to ask you to forgive me for making a fool of myself."

"That is all right, Ikey my boy," said Joe reaching out his hand to Ike, "it was your damned Indian blood."

Then we all settled down and talked about the cattle rustling situation, Joe and his hands and neighbors giving me all the information they could.

Before long it was time to do the feeding and cook supper.

So we all stayed with Joe a second night, and the next morning after breakfast we said good-by to Joe and Ike and took the trail for home.

I rode with Ed Tinker and stayed all night with him at his place.

The next morning I rode up to Caney, where I stayed awhile, trying to pick up information.

Then I went over to Coffeyville. There I put my pony in the livery barn and went to the Southern Hotel, which at that time was run by a man named Kohler.

He was a son of one of the men who had fired on the Dalton gang and killed two of them as they tried to make their getaway after the famous Coffeyville bank robbery.

INFORMATION WAS SCARCE

I had my supper and sat and listened to the talk going around but couldn't find out anything about the cattle stealing except that there was a lot of it going on.

I talked to some of the men and got the names of some fellows who were suspected and also of the men who had lost the most cattle.

In a couple of days I had about all the information I could get there, so I rode out of town.

After crossing Onion Creek I caught up with a bunch of cowboys who had been holding a herd down on 'Possum Creek. They had driven the cattle to Coffeyville just that morning and had put them into the shipping pens. Now they were on their way back to their camp.

I told the cowboys what my business was and they asked me to stay with them until they could get their cattle loaded that evening.

While they were loading, they said, I could look over the cattle in the stockyards. So I went to their camp with them.

While we were getting ready for dinner a freighter drove in and camped about fifty yards from us. He unhitched his team, made a fire, started his dinner cooking, and then he came over and sat down and started talking to us.

CROOKED DEPUTIES

While he was there one of the boys saw two deputy marshals come up to his wagon and, after looking all around, put a package into the wagon.

Then they rode away.

After they were out of sight we all went over to investigate.

The freighter took the package out of its hiding place and found it to be a quart of whisky.

"Well, I'll be damned," said the freighter. "That was kind of them." He took a drink; and the boys finished the bottle and threw it into the creek.

Then the freighter said, "Now, what do you suppose they did that for?"

"That's easy," I told him. "There's a law against taking whisky into the Indian Territory. The penalty is confiscation of your outfit and six months in the Fort Smith Federal Jail. The officer making the arrest gets three-fourths

of the money that the outfit sells for. Those two officers planted this evidence and will come back later and search your wagon. If it was still there they would take you in and Judge Parker would do the rest."

"Well," said the freighter, "they'll have a hell of a time producing that whisky! Do you think they really intended to do a dirty trick like that?"

"We will wait and see," I said. "There are some men in the world that are that low, and it's too bad that some of them are officers."

We all had dinner and the freighter was hitching up when, sure enough, the two marshals came riding back to his wagon.

The cowboys and I were watching. We all got on our ponies and rode over to listen. The two marshals told the freighter they would have to search his wagon to see if he was taking whisky into the Indian Territory.

245

The freighter said, "Search and be damned, gentlemen," and stepped back from the wagon.

The marshals searched and of course found no whisky.

The cowboys all gave them the horselaugh and, taking down their ropes, told the two officers what had happened.

Then they took the marshals' guns and threw them into the creek.

I got their names and promised to see that Judge Parker heard all about what they had tried to pull off.

Then the cowboys chased the two of them all the way back to the stockyards.

COW THIEF TAGS

That evening the boys drove their cattle into the cattle cars while I looked over the other stock in the pens.

Then we all went back to camp.

They asked me to stay with them and promised to help me find the rustlers.

The next day we spotted a beef wagon going into the hills. We gave them enough time to kill the beef and start dressing the meat; then we rode out on their trail.

When we came to the timbered hills the first thing we found was the rustlers' wagon. The harness was in the wagon but the horses and the rustlers were gone.

A little farther on we found the tracks of a large bunch of horsemen.

We followed the trail and it was not long before we came upon the rustlers hanging from the limb of a big cottonwood tree, each with a cow-thief tag pinned on his back. Their bodies were still warm, and for fear they might not be dead we let them hang there.

We had found our men, but the Vigilantes or the Lighthorse had found them first.

I sent my report to Captain Knipe and in a few days got a letter from him that there was nothing further on hand for me, so I could rest until some more complaints came in.

Soon after that I went down on Sand Creek and went to work for a man named Runyan who had raised a large crop of watermelons and was selling them to the traders. Runyan took from a hundred and fifty to two hundred watermelons on each load, down to the Osage Agency, while I stayed and took care of the place.

HORSE RACES AT JAKE BANKS'S

Jake Bartles ran a store on the Caney River just about where Bartlesville is now.

The store was both a business and social gathering place in those days.

On Saturday we always went up there to buy the things we needed and to visit with the people who came from far and near.

One Saturday there was going to be a big horse race at the race track across the river from the store, so Runyan and I got our work done up and rode over to see the race.

There was a crowd down from the States headed by the Roberts brothers, who had brought a race mare called the Jersey Heifer. She was a beautiful animal and looked every inch a racer.

The crowd from the States were backing her, to a man, with plenty of money.

247

The Territory boys were putting their money on a dark chestnut sorrel mare belonging to Edgar Halfmoon, a Delaware Indian. Robert Wheeler, also a Delaware, was riding her and he was a first-class rider.

The stakeholder, a tall, jolly sort of fellow, was a stranger in those parts who had come down from the States with the Roberts crowd. He drove a fine team and a brand new buggy and had left them on the other side of the river at Jake Bartles's store.

The stakes were five hundred dollars and all the side bets they could cover, so before long the stakeholder had more money than a bank.

Everyone had money on one horse or the other.

The distance was eight hundred yards. It was a straight track and was in first-class condition.

Jake Bartles and Sam Boaps were the judges, Sam at the starting line and Jake at the finish.

Everything was ready and they were waiting on the Roberts rider. They couldn't seem to get him started; he jacked (killed time) first one way and then another.

Finally they were off.

It was as pretty a race as you ever saw. They started even and ran that way for over half the distance; then Edgar Halfmoon's marc began to gain.

At six hundred yards she was head and neck in the lead and running smooth.

The Roberts rider laid on the buckskin but he couldn't catch her, and the game little thing came in ahead with two feet of daylight between herself and the Jersey Heifer.

The Territory boys went hog-wild, yelling and shooting their guns in the air.

One of the Roberts brothers made a speech congratulating the Territory boys on their winnings.

Then we all went to collect our bets.

George Keeler said he had seen the stakeholder go over to Jake Bartles's store, so we all went over to the store.

When we got there, we found that the stakeholder had got into his buggy a short time before and driven off down the Caney road as fast as his horses could go!

We looked at each other as the truth dawned. We remembered how the Roberts rider had delayed the start of the race . . . then the speech made by Roberts — all for the purpose of giving the stakeholder time to get a good start.

Charlie Nida, Jim Hymer and I started after him.

It was eighteen miles to Caney and we made it in an hour and forty minutes, only to find that he had changed teams and driven on.

No one seemed to know which road he had taken and we could not hire a fresh horse in the town.

We told the marshal what we thought of his town, its inhabitants, its officers and the whole state of Kansas.

Then we rested our horses and rode back home.

The boys we left at the store had got Roberts and were going to hang him but he had sworn he had lost as much as anyone and he had offered to chip in on a reward for the capture of the stakeholder, so after three or four fights they had turned him loose on his promise to catch the stakeholder if it was the last act of his life.

Some of the boys were not convinced and they still wanted to hang him but Jake Bartles, Sam Boaps and George Keeler talked them into letting Roberts go, although they thought there wasn't much doubt of his guilt.

Roberts went home that night a mighty lucky man to be alive.

I was still working for Runyan and we kept on selling melons until they were all gone; then we plowed the melon patch and fixed it up for a crop in the spring.

After we got the plowing done we went to husking corn and had the crop all out before the first of December — 1885.

We were taking it easy with only the feeding to do when the bad weather came.

We went to all the dances and the shooting matches and kept in trim for the big turkey match at Christmas time.

BOB GILSTRAP

Bob Gilstrap, the Cherokee Indian boy who was struck by lightning the night of the big storm up on Sand Creek, and Frank Linoe, a Delaware boy, had been working together in the Osage Nation.

Bob never did like to work and he would ride off and be gone for a week at a time while Linoe did all the work. Linoe finally finished, one time when Bob was gone, and drew the pay.

About that time Bob came back and wanted half of the money.

They quarreled and Bob drew his gun and took it all. Linoe told him that he would have a gun himself next time they met.

Bob went up to the Kaw Indian Agency and Linoe went to his home on Mission Creek and got his gun and started looking for Bob.

About that time there were some ponies stolen from the Big Hill Brands up near the Kaw Agency and just to be sure Bob didn't get into any trouble the Indian agent sent some Indian police after him.

They brought him back and locked him up but Bob wanted to go home for Christmas. His sister lived down by Jake Bartles's store and he wanted to have Christmas dinner with her. He begged so hard they finally let him go when he promised to be back before New Year's.

There was a big turkey shoot up at Johnstone and Keeler's across the river from Jake Bartles's store and Runyan and I had taken our rifles and gone up there. I had been shooting with a man named Ed Shipley and we had won ten turkeys and the store had run out of cigars so we went over to Jake Bartles to buy cigars for the crowd.

Frank Linoe and a man named Grant Ridenour were there and had been waiting all day for Bob to show up, but we didn't know the Indian agent had turned him loose.

As we came out of the store Bob came riding in and hitched his pony and walked over toward us. Linoe went out to meet him.

"Bob," said Linoe, "you threw your gun on me and took my money when I had no gun. I've got one now and so have you, so now we can settle it."

"Oh," said Bob, "I will get your money for you in a few days and we won't have to fight."

"Like hell you will!" said Linoe. "I don't want your money, I want your blood. Go for your gun! You got one— use it like you said you would out there in Osage."

"Yes," stalled Bob, "I've got a gun but I got no loads for it."

"Go in the store and get some," said Linoe, "they got them to sell."

"Sure," said Bob, "but I got no money."

For answer Linoe drew out a silver dollar and tossed it to him. Bob caught it, spit on it and threw it back in Linoe's face. "Keep your damned money and take it to hell with you," he yelled.

"Come on, you damned Delaware," and he walked into the store, Linoe at his heels with his gun in his hand.

Bob walked behind the counter and picked up a box of cartridges and began loading his gun.

Linoe was watching every move he made but before he had finished, the clerk, Harry Brent, took a sawed-off shotgun out from under the counter and, covering both of them, said, "Now, see here, boys, I don't give a damn how smoky you damn fools get but I want you to go outside to do it. If I have to clean up a mess of blood I'm going to be the one who makes it. I will put twenty-one buckshot in the first man that starts anything in here and I'm not playing any favorites. Go outside and fight all you please but if you pull a trigger in this store I will sure as hell kill both of you."

"Come on," Bob said to Linoe and started for the back door. Linoe followed.

The door opened outwards and had a glass top. Bob pushed the door open, slammed it shut in Linoe's face, and fired through the glass. Linoe fired back.

Then they each fired another shot.

The four shots came fast, almost a roar; we could hardly tell how many shots were fired.

Linoe was lying on some tobacco boxes inside the door and Bob was on the porch floor with his gun cocked for another shot but he didn't live long enough to pull the trigger.

He was stone dead when they picked him up. Linoe raised up and said, "I don't care a damn. He died first, anyhow." Then he fell back dead.

Harry Brent said, "Well, let's hang Ridenour now and call it a full day."

So we all went to look for Ridenour, but he was nowhere to be found and he never did come back again.

We loaded Bob in a wagon and took him across the river to his sister, Mrs. Keeler. She was standing in the yard, waiting, since she had heard the shooting and had guessed what had happened.

She was crying and said, "I saw Bob when he came past and I called to him to come in but he waved his hand and said he would be back. Who would have thought he would come back like this?" She broke down completely.

They sent a man with a spring wagon to Caney for a coffin. He got back before daylight and they buried Bob the next evening. Linoe's father came and took his body home up on Mission Creek.

There was bad feeling between the Cherokees and the Delawares over this fight for a long time and they all went around armed for a while, but there wasn't any more shooting.

ED WEBSTER'S

After we got all the corn husked and the stock field ready to turn the cattle in, I left Runyan and went to work for Ed Webster.

Ed had a spread up on Sand Creek and was buying and selling Western ponies. He had about a hundred head and my job was looking after them.

253

When he sold one, he let the buyer pick his pony out of the herd, then I would rope and ride it for him. Some days I would ride as many as ten or twelve; other times a week would pass and I would ride only one or two, just enough to keep in practice.

The rest of the time I spent up at the bunkhouse with the other boys.

We played poker and seven-up and sat around and talked.

Sometimes we went hunting. One day after a deep snow the boys wanted to go deer hunting. So after the feeding was done we took our rifles and went.

We hunted all day and saw plenty of signs of deer but Dave McMillen was the only one who got one.

ED WEBSTER AND ME
WEBSTER RANCH SANO CREEK, CHEROKEE NATION 1887

Ed Webster came down to the bunkhouse and called me over. "Listen, Frank," he said, "I'm going up to Independence and get married. I may be gone a week or I may stay six months. I am going to turn everything over to you and you run it like you would your own. Sell all the ponies you can and I will leave you money to pay the boys and buy the grub."

254

Who is the girl?" asked Dave McMillen, who was standing near.

"She is Hattie Bennett," said Ed, "though I don't think it's any of your damned business."

By that time all the boys had gathered around and were wishing him the best of everything and he forked his pony and rode off amid the shouts from the boys.

Ed was gone six weeks.

He and his bride rode in one afternoon when we were all out so I didn't know they were home until after sundown.

I rode up to the house to make my report for I had sold a lot of ponies and had twenty-six hundred dollars for the boss.

They called to me to come in.

Ed had gone to bed and Hattie was combing her hair in front of the mirror.

Ed had taken off his tie, a long spotted one, and thrown it on the foot of the bed. It had fallen on the floor in a coil with one end sticking out. Turning from the mirror as I came in, Hattie saw the tie and thought it was a rattlesnake.

She screamed, "Oh, my God, Ed, there's a big rattlesnake on the bed! Lie still and don't move."

"Like hell I will," yelled Ed, and he threw the covers and landed in the middle of the room.

Then he saw what had frightened her and crawled back into bed again.

After we got through laughing I gave Ed his money and went back to the bunkhouse. I told the boys that Ed was home and about the necktie snake and we all had a good laugh.

The next day we got word to all the neighbors and that night they came from near and far to a party for the newlyweds.

Someone brought a fiddler and we danced until daylight.

Ed had plenty of refreshments and everybody had a wonderful time.

TROUBLE DOWN THE CREEK

Things had been pretty quiet for a while when one day Dave Overacker came riding down and told us there was trouble down the creek.

A man had rented a farm from Jasper Exendine and brought his wife and three children down from the States. They were nice-looking people, all of them.

After they got settled the man got an idea in his head that he could marry an Indian woman and take a farm of his own.

He laid the plan before his wife. She was to leave him, and after he married the Indian woman and got the farm improved he would do away with her and his wife could come back and they would have the farm.

His wife would not agree to the plan so he told her he was going to kill her and get an Indian woman anyway.

He went after her with an iron rod and beat her until he thought she was dead. Then he started on his children.

Dave Thornton had been to the store and was just riding by the place when he heard the children screaming.

He rode up to the house to see what was the trouble. The man lit out, but the children ran to Dave and told him what had happened. Dave sent the children after Jasper Exendine while he himself went into the house. There he found the woman was still alive.

When Jasper came, he and Dave tried to revive her but couldn't; so Dave went after his wife to help them. When the two of them got back, the woman had come to and was telling Jasper how it all had started.

As soon as the woman was able to go, Dave's wife took her and the three children home.

Jasper got on his pony and started down the creek to gather up a posse.

He stopped at Dave Overacker's, so then Dave came up the creek to tell the cowpunchers at Ed Webster's. By the time he had finished his story Ed and all the boys were ready and we rode over to Happen's ranch and were joined by his boys.

Then we went on to Charlie Nida's and got his crowd and before sundown there was a posse of armed men at Jasper Exendine's, ready for business.

We went up to the renter's house and found the door locked and the windows all covered. It looked as if the damned fool was in there and ready for a fight.

We surrounded the house and put three men at each window and some more at the back door. I was at the front door with Jasper Exendine, Charlie Nida, Dave Overacker and Ed Webster.

We knocked and called but got no answer. So Jasper burst the door open with his shoulder and we went in. We found the man had got ready for a battle, but had apparently changed his mind and left.

He had not been gone long, so we all remounted and started after him.

We rode fast and were not far behind him when we reached the ford in the river.

We found by his tracks that he had taken the road to Caney from there and we took after him.

As we came out of the timber on Post Oak Creek we saw him not two hundred yards ahead. When he heard our horses he looked around and saw us and there was just a streak of man and horse half a mile long.

The chase was on.

He had a fresher horse and held his lead for about a mile; then we began closing in on him.

He fired back at us but didn't hit anything and the boys fanned out.

When he saw he was losing he left the trail and tried to reach the timber.

Charlie Nida, Lee Keyes, Ed Webster and I were on the timber side of him, almost even, and closing in with our ropes down, ready to catch him.

As he came on, in a desperate effort to reach the timber, not a hundred yards away, he fired the last shots from his gun, not thirty feet away — and missed.

Bending down to dodge our ropes, he made his try for life.

I was in the lead and was swinging my rope to make the catch when my horse stepped in a hole and turned a somersault.

When I came to I was lying by a fire and the boys were all around me. My head felt as big as a salt barrel and my face was cut up as if I had been fighting wildcats. I raised up and asked, "Did you get him, boys?"

"Well," said Ed Webster, "the last I saw of him he was looking up into a tree, pulling on a lariat, without a toehold. He had hold of the rope with his neck and his hands were tied behind him."

Our horses were tired and we rode home slowly.

We got there a little after sunrise and when we had looked after the stock we lay around and slept.

About the time I had fully recovered from my fall I had a letter from Captain Knipe with orders to go down on the Caney River, where they were having trouble with cattle rustlers.

18 TIME CATCHES UP

CAPTAIN William "Bill" A. Knipe was head of the Cattlemen's Association in the Indian Territory; later he took a claim in Oklahoma and started the town of Perkins. He was an important political figure in the Indian Territory and early Oklahoma statehood, and was a friend and firm supporter of the first governor, George W. Steele.

Captain Knipe had a ranch, the Bar Triangle, down on the Caney River, where they had been having trouble with cattle rustlers.

I was still a troubleshooter for the Cattlemen's Association so he sent me down there to help his men find the rustlers.

The Bar Triangle was a small spread but the captain had some fine cattle and horses and he didn't like the idea of some rustler shipping them out. He had a reputation of making it smoky for any man he caught, so the rustlers were afraid of him and his hired men and usually let him pretty much alone. That time they seemed to be determined to make off with some of his cattle.

After the rustler situation was in hand I stayed on at the Bar Triangle as a hand and Captain Knipe sent me and another rider by the name of Clint Meeks down to his camp at the mouth of Double Creek.

We were to ride after the cattle down there and look after a bunch of cows he was trying to fatten.

One day we had just finished hauling the feed to the stock when the supply wagon came in from the ranch and the driver told us that the Roberts gang had been down from the States to fix up a horse race at the track down at Cap Bain's.

They had posted a fifty-dollar forfeit bet on a horse race to be run in two weeks and were bringing a horse to race one of Cap Bain's racers.

THE PAY-OFF HORSE RACE

This was the best chance in the world to get even with them for getting away with the money at the race up at Jake Bartles's store.

Clint and I sat around and made war medicine until after midnight and had things pretty well thought out.

The next day we rode up to see Captain Knipe and he agreed to our plan.

We got all the money we could and spread the news.

When the time came Clint and I filled our feed troughs and hay racks so full that we could stay all night and an extra day if we had to. We oiled our guns, took a fresh box of shells, saddled our horses and started way before daylight on the day before the race.

On the day of the race, before the Roberts gang got in, all the boys knew what each one was expected to do.

Roberts came in about the middle of the forenoon. He had a team and buggy and about six or eight men besides the stakeholder. They had two racehorses and a whole sack of money.

There was a crowd of about two hundred people, all-betting freely.

The stakeholder had a sack of wagers and was smiling like a 'possum eating yellow jackets.

I kept away from the Roberts gang along with some of the boys who had been at the other race.

We watched the stakeholder and laughed about the surprise that was in store for him.

Cap Bain's youngest son, Fletcher, was riding his dad's racer. He was light and a good rider and we all knew that if his mount was the fastest it would come in first, for he always rode to win.

WE WERE READY!

Charlie Nida, Lee Keyes and his father, Chancey Bain, Runyan and I were up in the barn loft watching the stakeholder, who was standing just below us, by his buggy, taking bets.

After the Territory boys had all their money up the crowd, all but the stakeholder started out to the racetrack, about a mile from the house.

We sat in the barn loft and waited.

Pretty soon one of the Roberts men came back and he and the stakeholder started to hitch the team to the buggy.

Pulling our handkerchiefs up over our faces, we dropped down and covered them. We took the sack of money they had collected, tied their hands and gagged them with strips cut from the lap robe; then we took them down into the timber and tied each of them to a tree.

We went back and got the team with the buggy and drove them to the edge of the timber where they had fifteen miles of open road ahead of them.

We tied the lines and hung them over the dashboard and hit each horse and started them running toward home.

Then we took the money sack up to the house and left it while we went out to the racetrack to watch the horses run.

Roberts was at the starters' line with big Joe Carter. Cap Bain and another Roberts's man were at the finish line. It was the best horse race that had ever been run on that track.

Both riders laid on the buckskin but it was a dead heat and had to be run over again.

They raced again and it was a good race, too. Fletcher Bain came in a neck ahead and the Territory boys went wild.

They all went back to the house to collect their winnings.

When they got there they found the stakeholder and his team and buggy gone and no one knew where they went. The boys and I were ready. "Well," I said, "this is twice you have done this trick and we think it's about time you quit it."

The boys all gathered around Roberts and the three men who were with him and disarmed them.

The Roberts rider and another of their men had made their getaway and were hightailing it for the state line. They were pushing on their bridle reins and looking behind them for dust.

Roberts was allowed to plead his case for his men and himself.

We elected Cap Bain Judge, and Parson Evans was the prosecutor.

There were plenty of witnesses to tell how they had done the same thing at Jake Bartles's store.

I told how we had ridden after the stakeholder, that time, and lost him at Caney, Kansas.

We all told how Jake Bartles and Sam Boaps got Roberts off and kept the boys from hanging him.

"Well," said Cap Bain, "Sam and Jake are not here now to get these men off so we will just lock them in the smokehouse and adjourn till we can give them what they have coming."

We tied them up and put them into the smokehouse.

When the four men were taken care of we went into the house and told Mrs. Bain about it. We just wanted to give them a good scare, so we got her to help us and we told her what to do.

Mrs. Bain took the butcher knife and went out to the smokehouse pretending to be after some bacon for supper.

The Roberts men began trying to bribe her to cut them loose. She stalled around as we had told her to do and finally accepted one hundred and forty dollars.

She cut the ropes and told them she would tie their horses back of the smokehouse and unlock the door and they could make a run for the horses.

Taking her money she came back where we were waiting and reported.

Some of the boys went out and got on their ponies to hide along the road and give them a good start.

Mrs. Bain tied the horses where the men could get to them and told them to hurry for the men might hang her if they found out what she had done.

Then she went into the house where we were waiting and we all watched the Roberts men sneak out of the smokehouse and get on their horses.

Then we all ran out of the house and started shooting in the air but we let them pass, and the first race of the day was no comparison to the last one. They really tore out for the state line.

After getting them well on their way we went down through the timber and found the stakeholder and his buddy still tied to their trees. There had been a lot of ants in the stakeholder's tree and they had come out and bit him. His arms and legs were badly swollen from the ropes but he could still talk and the way he cussed us would have made a bullwhacker envious.

That stakeholder had a fine command of language and he used it all.

Cap Bain looked very serious and said it was a shame to hang a man who had such a fine vocabulary and we should not destroy such a fountain of profanity and have it lost to the world.

He ordered us to put the men on their horses, bareback, tie each man's feet under his horse's belly and start them up the trail so they could carry their story as a warning to other crooks.

The last we saw of them they were going up the trail cussing the Territory and everyone in it and vowing to come back and Idll all of us.

After supper Cap Bain got the money sack out and gave each man his money and his winnings and there was enough left over to pay the boys what they had lost on the race at Jake Bartles's store.

After we were all settled up there was still some money left so we played poker for it and it got into the pockets of nearly all the boys before Mal Beeson finally cinched it and kept it as the game broke up.

The next morning after breakfast Clint and I went back to the Bar Triangle.

BELLE STARR

It was in the middle '8o's then, just about the time Winchesters were getting plentiful.

I was riding across the prairie in the Cherokee Nation one day when I saw a lady rider coming toward me.

She was wearing a long black riding skirt and a large white Stetson hat. As she came closer I saw it was Belle Starr.

I had known Belle for years. She was a very hospitable person and loved company; I had stopped at her house often.

266

When we met on the prairie we pulled up our horses and shook hands. She was riding a pretty sorrel-red horse and I was admiring him.

Belle said, "Yes, he is pretty and he can outrun anything in this part of the country."

"You forget, don't you, that I am riding old Tex?" Old Tex was buckskin and he was fast.

"That doesn't make any difference," said Belle, "my horse can choke old Tex to death with forty feet of rope at four hundred yards."

I doubted that. "I don't believe it." I bet my Winchester against her belt gun, a slicker and three blankets.

There were no trails on the prairie but we rode out to a place where the grass was not so high so the horses could run and took off our hats and threw them down for a stopping place, then we rode across the prairie to what we estimated to be about two hundred yards.

Belle's horse was a fast breaker and she got off to a better start than I did.

That old black skirt of Belle's flew clear behind her horse's tail. I know, for I was looking at her from behind.

She outran me by ten feet of daylight.

I pulled out the Winchester and gave it to her.

It was a model 1873 forty-four forty. Belle said, "I want the holster, too."

"Hold on, I didn't bet the holster."

"I know," said Belle, laughing, "but wouldn't you look funny with a holster and no gun?"

I took it off and helped her put the outfit on her saddle.

She used it after that, and that is the gun that is known as "Belle Starr's famous Winchester."

It now belongs to the collection of Fred Sutton in Oklahoma City, Oklahoma.

I remember the night Belle was killed. We were all at a dance in a house down at Younger Bend.

A fellow by the name of Edgar Watson was there; he was stuck on Belle and wanted to take her home.

It was time for the last dance and I was dancing with her. We were standing on the floor waiting for the music to begin when he came out and asked her again if he could take her home.

She said, "No, I can make it by myself, I always have."

I guess Watson thought I was going to take her home, but I wasn't.

He left the dance right then and rode out about two hundred yards to where she would have to cross the creek.

There he waited.

After the dance Belle left ahead of the rest of us and when she came to the creek she stopped to let her horse drink.

She was just sitting there waiting when Edgar shot her from his hiding place.

She fell off her horse and the horse came running back.

We heard the shot and ran for the ford in the creek.

When we got there we could hear Watson's horse running off through the timber so we started on his trail.

We chased him nearly one hundred miles.

He knew the country and he took the timber, streams and sheltered places.

He was never very far ahead of us; once we had a gunfight with him but it was getting dark and we lost him gain in the timber.

After three weeks of steady tracking we caught up with him on the prairie down in the eastern part of the Creek Nation.

His horse was killed in the gun battle that followed, but we took him alive. And Belle Starr's friends hung her killer to a tree with her own lariat.

BLUEBIRD, THE CHEYENNE

It was about the year 1887.

I was down on Gray Horse Creek working for Dan Modene.

We were camped at Gray Horse Station.

Bert Smith was one of the hands and one day he and I went down to see an Indian friend of ours, called "Old Blackbird." He was a good Indian and lived down on the creek not far from where we were camped.

When we got there he had a visitor, a Cheyenne Indian named Bluebird; a big fellow with a mean look in his eye.

Bluebird was telling tales of Indian warfare and bragging about some of the dirty tricks he had played, several years before when he had worked for the government as a scout.

In those days there were forts throughout the country where soldiers were stationed to protect the people from lawless elements and Indian uprisings.

269

Scouts were sent out by the soldiers to keep them informed about hostile Indians and what they were doing.

It must have been in the early '70's when Bluebird was a scout.

He told about laying an ambush of Sioux and Cheyenne Indians; then going back to the fort and telling the soldiers he had found some Indian trails.

When the soldiers went with him to investigate the trails he led them right to the ambush, where they were slaughtered without a chance.

Bert Smith and I listened as Bluebird told his tales. Evil tales of attacks on wagon trains and lonely cabins. . . How the Indians scalped and murdered their victims . . . He talked on and on. Indian fighting was rugged in those days.

One of Bluebird's stories was about the massacre of General Custer and his soldiers in the battle on the Little Big Horn.

General Custer arrived at night at the junction of the Big Horn and Little Big Horn rivers and discovered the Indians who were massed there under the leadership of Sitting Bull, but his scouts mistook them for a bunch of Pawnees known to be on their way to join Sitting Bull.

The Indians were on a ridge west of the Little Big Horn and when morning came, General Custer and his soldiers forded the river and rode for the Indian line.

A rise, across the stream, hid many of the Indians as they lay in wait between the river and the higher ridge beyond.

As Custer crossed the stream they rode against him and swarmed around to his rear.

Greatly outnumbered, the soldiers still fought their way up the ridge and a few of them with their general reached it.

Then a fresh band of Sioux and Cheyenne Indians rose up, led by the Sioux Chief Rain-in-the-Face, and not a man was left alive.

Bluebird was one of the Cheyennes and he took part in the massacre.

It is a matter of history that General Custer was not scalped when he was killed.

According to the Cheyenne, the general had killed four men with his saber in hand-to-hand combat, before he went down.

So General Custer was not scalped, for the Indians believed it was bad luck to scalp a man who had killed even two men with his sword before he himself was killed.

Bluebird stood beside the logs at the fireplace and showed us how, after the general was dead, Rain-in-the- Face stood over General Custer, cut his heart out and carried it into the camp with his teeth; for he believed that the heart of such a brave man as General Custer would bring more bravery to him.

Bluebird told about torturing the wounded men on the battlefield after the fight was over.

One man he scalped didn't die so he cut strips of flesh down his back. But still he didn't die. He cut off his ears and gouged out his eyes with the point of his knife; he cut more strips from the soldier's back and kept this up until he did die.

I looked at Bert and we went out together.

It was winter. The air outside was cold and frosty and clean.

Bert and I decided that Cheyenne had lived too damned long!

I DREW THE FOOT LOG

There was a dance that night on the other side of the creek and Bluebird, the Cheyenne, was going over.

We decided to wait until he came back.

There were two logs that made the bridges across the creek.

One was a foot log that crossed the creek right there at Old Blackbird's place. The other was down the creek a ways, at a ford crossing.

The foot log was the one that was nearest to the dance and the logical way for Bluebird to come back, so Bert and I both wanted to wait for him there.

Well, we had a deck of cards so we settled it by cutting the cards for the foot log. I was high man so I won and Bert got the log at the ford down the creek.

We took up our stations early, and I thought that Cheyenne was mine! But before midnight it began to sleet and the foot log got pretty slick.

I waited.

It was cold and the log got slicker all the time.

A couple of hours after midnight I heard two shots down by the ford!

I had waited a long time for that Cheyenne. It was cold sitting there with my gun cocked and aimed at that slippery log. So I went back to Old Blackbird's.

Bert Smith came in about the same time I did; he was cold too.

It was funny about those two shots; Bert should have got that Indian with one shot. But then, he was cold from sitting there so long and it was dark too.

Bert didn't say anything about seeing him and naturally I didn't ask; I looked at his gun, but of course we didn't always notch our guns for Indians in those days.

I watched him as he walked across the room and held his hands to the fire. There was a smile of satisfaction on his face, and we never saw the Cheyenne again!

19 OLD OKLAHOMA

I BUY A CLAIM

OLD Oklahoma was opened to homesteaders April 22, 1889. Charlie Devore and Ed Webster had then staked claims down on the Cimarron River.

Ed sold his claim and later Charlie wanted to sell his, too, so I decided to buy it.

I traded him a cow and a calf and a yearling heifer for his relinquishment, and I filed on the place October 6, 1889.

Charlie Nida went in with me, and together we cut and hewed a set of house logs and put up the first hewed-log house in that part of the country.

We cut a big red oak tree and made clapboards and covered it and we had the only house in those parts that didn't leak. We chinked and plastered it with red clay and were ready to move in by the middle of November.

TARANTULA AND TOAD

One day Charlie and I were sitting under a tree resting when we saw some weeds moving. We thought it might be a snake so we went out to see.

We sneaked up to the weeds and looked over the tall grass. In a little clearing was a toad and a tarantula fighting like the devil.

The tarantula wasn't very large, just about as big around as a pint cup, but the toad was pretty good-sized.

Every little while the toad would stop fighting and go over and eat a few bites of a weed. He always went back to the same weed and ate just a few of the leaves, then he would go back and fight some more.

The tarantula would just stand there and wait until he came back.

The fight wasn't getting anywhere and Charlie and I wanted to see more action so Charlie said to the toad, "Get in there and fight, darn you. Quit stopping to eat and do your fightin'," and he pulled up the little weed and threw it away.

Pretty soon the toad came back for another bite of the leaves. He looked around for the little weed but it was gone. He hopped around frantically, looking for the weed, then he fell over and in less than half a minute he was stone dead.

Charlie and I looked at each other. Not until then had we realized that the little weed was an antidote for the tarantula's poison.

We both felt terrible and would have given anything to undo what we had done. We searched everywhere for the little weed, but the grass was high and there were all kinds of weeds so we couldn't find it.

We two ignorant human beings had stood there and that little toad had shown us a remedy that might have helped all mankind, but we could not even recognize God's handiwork!

TO THE CHEROKEE NATION

As soon as the house was finished Charlie and I took a team and wagon and went back to the Cherokee Nation after our things.

In a few days we had gathered up our be-longings and started for home.

We were driving through the Osage Nation and were looking for some stock, so we went down to the spring, Nelagoney.

Its name, in the Osage language, means "good water."

OUTLAWS ON PAUL AIKEN CREEK

When we went around the hill at the Osage Agency a posse of United States officers was camped there and Jasper Exendine, who was with them, came out and hailed us.

"Boys," he said, "there is a bunch of outlaws, led by a man named Jackson, camped down on Paul Aiken Creek.

They have been robbing post offices up in the States and coming down into the Osage Nation to hide out. They have terrorized the country with their killing and cattle stealing and we have to go after them. We need you to come with us."

We had our gun belts on and of course we had our rifles with us. Charlie had his Winchester forty-four forty and I had a Winchester Express fifty ninety-five that shot an explosive bullet.

The officers had two wagons and we joined them.

We went on down to Paul Aiken Creek and scouted the lay of the land. On the opposite side of the creek was a house, and there the outlaws were hiding out.

The cabin was made of logs, was about twenty steps up from the creek, and behind the house was a cow lot.

Around the house were about forty acres of corn and the whole layout was surrounded by steep limestone bluffs.

The only way in or out was to cross the creek.

Right at the house the water was deep, the finest hole of water in the country, but about two hundred yards down the creek from the house there was a riffle where we could walk across stepping from one rock to another.

We picked out a campsite about one half-mile below the riffle, around the point of a hill, where the outlaws could not see us.

In the east side of the cornfield there was a big rock that had rolled down from the top of the bluff. It was about the size of a two-story house and it had been there so long that weeds and shrubbery had grown up all around it.

There was a fence around the cornfield and the cattle had made a trail around the rock and the fence.

I was scouting that side of the field and was walking cautiously around the rock when I came to a sharp turn, so I flattened myself against the rock.

Then I stuck my head out — and looked right into the muzzles of five rifles.

There they were, all five of them, with their rifles at their hips. They had been watching us and had me covered all the time.

They were Ernest Lewis and his brother Bill, the man called Jackson and two men I didn't know.

Ernest Lewis greeted me with, "Morning, sir, which way you going?"

I turned around and put the rock between us as fast as I could, yelling over my shoulder, "Back to camp, by God!"

They all whooped, and then I whooped and gobbled!

You know what that means!

No?

That is a call of defiance— it means somebody is going to die!

When we were out on the prairie and heard an Indian whoop and gobble we didn't answer unless we were ready and wanted to fight.

Well, the men were prepared to fight. They left the other side of the rock and went down to the house and got ready.

They hung blankets over the windows, leaving a crack at the bottom to shoot through.

It was about ten o'clock in the morning when the fight got started. The posse had come in and were lying along the creek bank, by the field fence and out in the milk lot.

There were about fifteen of them all told. Lafe Shadley was the head marshal in charge of the posse.

"Better come out and give up, boys. You can't get away!" Shadley called out.

"We are not coming," answered Ernest Lewis. "Suppose you try coming after us."

"We are going to get you."

"There will be a lot of new faces in hell when we get there!" was the only answer.

Somebody shot, I don't know who.

We just shot back and forth once in a while.

After a while one of our men named Jasper stuck his head up and Ernest Lewis called out, "Stick your old bald head up a little higher and I'll part your hair for you."

We hadn't got mad yet and nobody was shooting to kill.

By the middle of the afternoon there wasn't as much shooting but it was more dangerous. Both sides were getting down to business.

After about an hour by sun Ernest Lewis called out, "Frank, are you there?"

"Yes, what do you want?"

"Wish you would turn the cows in with the calves. My business is so damn confining I can't come out."

"All right," I said, "don't shoot, I'm coming over the bank."

I leaned my rifle up against a tree and went over the bank.

"Come up to the house and get a bucket and milk me a bucket of milk," said Ernest. "I'm going to churn about Saturday."

"If you take the milk where you are going it's going to be so hot it will sour before Saturday," I told him.

Ernest opened the door and told me to come in. I stepped inside and made a mental picture of the inside of the room.

All the men were there.

There were only two rooms in the house and no door between. The men were at the windows with their rifles ready. In the center of the room were two or three Winchesters, a number of shotguns and an arsenal of ammunition arranged in different piles for the different guns.

In the corner of the room was a forty-gallon wooden barrel, full of water, with some tin cups hanging on the outside. The barrel was about six feet from the window.

There was a cook stove and a big pile of stove wood.

They looked to be pretty well fixed for a long siege.

280

Logs and rocks were piled under the windows to protect the men lying there with their rifles and the room was dim enough so a man could not be sky lighted between the windows.

They were war wise all right.

I took it all in as Ernest handed me the bucket and I backed out of the door.

I went out to the cow lot and let down the bars and let the cows in to the calves, then started milking. When the bucket was full I let the calves finish sucking, then hollered to Ernest, "You want me to turn the cows out and leave the calves in the pen?"

"Yes, turn them out; I want fresh milk in the morning," he called back.

On the other side of the house the shooting was pretty brisk and I hollered to Ernest, "Hold on with that shooting till I deliver this milk and get over the bank again!"

Ernest laughed and said, "Come on in and let them shoot; they ain't hurtin' anything."

"I know," I said, "but some of our boys might shoot clear through the house and get me."

"Wouldn't that be hell!" said Ernest.

ALL FRIENDSHIP CEASES

I handed the milk through the door and Ernest gave me a letter and asked me to give it to his wife when I went to town.

I took the letter and he put out his hand.

We shook hands, and he said, "Now, here is where all friendship ceases. Get over the bank and do your damnedest."

I had never had any trouble with the two Lewis boys. In fact, we had always been friends. They were brave men and good shots. They were outlaws, but their word was good and in those days that was the measure of a man.

I said, "So long," and jumped over the bank, and Ernest fired a shot right over me to let me knew the truce was over.

I had been using a spare forty-four the marshals had in their wagon. Now I took it back to camp and got my old Express rifle with the exploding bullet.

Coming back up the creek, I hid myself behind a clump of trees on the opposite side of the creek about one hundred yards from the house.

I thought I was smart and they wouldn't be looking for me on that side of the creek.

I judged back from the window where I thought the water barrel was standing and took aim at about what I thought would be the bottom of the barrel. I wanted to let all the water out with one shot.

But I forgot about the smoke from my powder.

No sooner had my gun fired than they all took a few shots at me. I didn't have very good protection so I went down the creek bank and then up again to get as close to the house as I could.

Lying as near the top of the creek bank as I dared, I took aim at the hole I had already made and commenced to space-shoot all around it. I heard somebody in the house cussing; then lead got so thick I didn't dare draw a long breath.

I just faded away from there and hunted safer quarters.

Shadley divided us up then, and part of us went back to camp to eat supper. Then we stood guard while the other boys ate. When they came back we all lay down right where we were and stayed there all night.

Everything was quiet all night. That's why we had to watch so close.

But in the morning one of our boys stuck his head up over the creek bank and lost his hat, so we knew they were still there and ready for action.

After a while Ernest Lewis hollered at me again. "Frank, will you milk us some more milk this morning?"

"Sure!" I hollered back. "Hold your fire!" And I got up and started for the kitchen door.

When he opened the door to give me the bucket I looked to see what I had done.

That barrel was a total wreck!

They had caught a few bucketfuls of water and the dishpan and wash pan were full. They had them setting on the floor right behind the wreck of the old barrel.

Gunpowder smoke makes a man awful thirsty, and they had used a lot of water so they didn't have much left.

As Ernest handed me the bucket he said, "Just leave the bars down so the cows and calves can get out. I don't expect to need any more milk for a while."

I let the cows out and milked the bucket full.

When I handed it back through the door Ernest said, "Well, so long, Frank. You think you've got us, and maybe you have. But let's be men about it. I'm going to part your hair right down the center if I can!"

THE BREAK

I got back over the bank and we talked over the situation. We knew they were going to make a break, for they were getting low on water.

There was a timbered gulch running up into the bluffs on the east side of the cornfield; it was the logical place for them to make for.

I took up my watch in a cedar tree, behind a big rock, about five hundred yards from the house, with my rifle aimed at the fence they would have to get over before they made the timber.

About noon they made the break.

They split up — and Ernest Lewis and his brother and another man made the creek.

But our boys had them surrounded and covered, so they gave up without firing a shot.

Jackson and the other man made for the gulch on outside of the house.

In the cornfield below me was a Cherokee Indian named Al Landis.

He was lying on his rifle and when he saw the two men coming he jumped up and ran to meet them, trying to head them off.

They were running toward each other with their rifles at their hips, firing as they ran, each in too big a hurry to take aim.

In the volley of shots the other man was killed.

Jackson slowed down. Then he started right toward Landis, shaking the lead out of his gun as he went.

Everyone stopped shooting and just stood up and watched.

Jackson raised his right arm to take aim and as he did Landis got him in the right wrist and shattered his upper arm at the same time.

Jackson reached for his gun with his left hand but Landis was close enough to strike him with his rifle barrel on the side of his head and knock him out.

Jackson and the dead man were taken to Bartlesville. There Jackson's arm was amputated.

Ernest Lewis and his brother and the other man were taken to the Federal Prison at Guthrie.

LEWIS ESCAPES

The night after the men were lodged in prison at Guthrie, Ernest Lewis broke out and let all the other prisoners out. So, with a lot of new recruits, he was back in operation again.

On Saturday about a week later I was in Jake Bartles's store talking to Al Landis when Lee Keyes came in and told me a man outside wanted to see me.

I went out and Ernest Lewis got off his horse and stood by the hitch rack.

"You got any papers you want to serve?" he asked.

"Not for you," I said.

"You haven't got a warrant for me?"

"Not right now, I haven't. Why?" I asked.

"I just wanted to know," he said. "I know you always believe in fair play and I didn't want you to take a hand against me unless you had to. Landis is in there, isn't he?"

"Yes, he is."

"He got Jackson," he said, "but I just wanted you to see that an Indian won't stand up to a white man."

Landis was standing inside with his rifle resting on his toe, his hand around the breech and through the lever, his finger on the trigger and his thumb on the hammer.

I went in the front door and Lewis went in the side door, at the same time. He was pulling off his gloves as he went in.

"Hello, Lewis, when did you get in?" A man named Keeler spoke up.

"Oh, I've been here a little while," he answered. "Why, there's Al Landis. I have a ring in my pocket I've been going to put in his nose."

He put his left hand in his left pocket, never moving his right hand, which hung loose at his side right over his gun.

Then he said, "Well, I haven't got the ring. Guess I'll have to tie a string around his neck."

"Stay where you are, Lewis," said Landis. "Don't try to come any nearer."

But Lewis kept walking right on up to him and fumbling with his left hand as if he were hunting for a string.

Landis was backing toward the door with his rifle in his hand; all he had to do was raise it and fire, but instead he broke and ran!

He got on his horse and rode for the marshals' camp.

Lewis turned to me, "Didn't I tell you?" he said.

Then he bought cigars for the crowd.

Lewis turned to Keeler and asked, "Where are they holding Jackson?"

"Over at the hotel," said Keeler. "Shadley and a couple of marshals are guarding him."

The Keelers ran the hotel where the officers were holding Jackson.

"Guess I'll go over and see him," said Lewis.

"Be careful, Lewis, don't start any trouble over there," said Keeler.

"There ain't a damn bit of danger, George," said Lewis, starting out the door.

Keeler and I followed him over and into the hotel.

Lewis went down the hall looking for Jackson's room.

The door was open and he walked in. "Howdy, gentlemen," he said politely. "Will you just stand over on the other side of the room? I came to see Jackson."

Shadley and his two men stood over on the other side of the room back of the bed. Lewis grinned.

"It's dangerous to play with loaded guns, boys, and I see you are all wearing them."

Then he turned to Jackson. "Hello, Jackson, how you feeling?"

"Pretty tough."

"You won't be able to travel for three weeks but I will send one of the boys in and you let me know when you are ready. Then we will come and get you."

After visiting a little while with Jackson, Lewis turned his back on the three marshals and walked out of the room.

But his hand was on his hat brim and he was looking at them in a mirror on his wrist; if one of them had gone for his gun Lewis was ready and they knew it.

Charlie Nida and I gathered up our stock and started back home.

When we got to the Osage Agency — it was called Pawhuska by that time — we camped and put our stock in the livery stable at the wagon yard.

We were just leaving the livery barn when I saw Charlie Pettit walking up to me. Charlie was a big Negro Deputy United States Marshal, from the Wichita Court.

"Frank," he said, "Ernest Lewis is up at the hotel and I have a warrant for him. He may have a gang up there. Come up and help me get him."

We started up to the hotel together.

Lewis was sitting on the porch. He started like he was going to make a gunplay, but I put my hand on my gun and shook my head at him and he stopped.

He and I had played with guns and he knew I was the best shot.

"Sorry, Mr. Lewis," Pettit said, "but I have a warrant for you and it's a fugitive warrant."

By that he meant that Lewis was paid for if anything went wrong. He had committed a crime that was punishable by death. Pettit's orders were to bring him in dead or alive.

"Unbuckle your gun belt carefully and drop your gun," Pettit told him.

Lewis unbuckled his gun and handed the whole outfit to me.

Pettit reached for his handcuffs and just then the whole window burst out on him with shotgun shells.

288

I covered Lewis and started for the door and at the same time Pettit went in through the window.

Inside the window stood Lewis's wife with a gun in her hands! She had shot both barrels of the shotgun at once and blown the whole window clear out onto the porch floor.

Pettit grabbed the gun barrel, then saw it was a woman.

"Madam," he said taking off his hat, "them things get a person hurt. You should be more careful."

Pettit put his handcuffs on Mrs. Lewis and my handcuffs on Ernest. He took his prisoners to Guthrie, where he put them in the Federal jail.

They stayed there almost a week, that time, but then broke out again and left the country for good.

Charlie Nida and I loaded our wagon and tied our saddle ponies behind and started for home.

We crossed the Arkansas River at Jim McCame's ferry at the mouth of Gray Horse Creek and were well on the way to the Pawnee Agency when it started to rain.

We knew that if we didn't get across Black Bear Creek at the Pawnee Agency we would have to lay over till the water went down.

There was no telling when that would be, so we just kept driving to get across before the creek got too high.

We reached the Black Bear about the middle of the afternoon and got across.

The water was up to the wagon box and running swiftly. Both banks of the creek were full of wagons and teams.

We stopped on a little knoll on the south bank and made camp.

We had a large tent, about twelve by eighteen, that we put up; in a short time we had a fire in one end and the horses tied at the other end eating their hay.

We carried in some driftwood and then sat down on our blankets to smoke and enjoy ourselves. But it kept on raining and some of the outfits had no shelter, so we told them to come into our tent to dry.

Before sundown there were six women and men and nine little children in the tent —so they cooked their supper and brought in their blankets, and Charlie and I slept with the horses and let them have the rest of the tent.

The next morning it was still raining. There were no roads and the mud was bottomless. The wagons were all loaded and it was hard for them to proceed in the rain.

We all stayed over another day.

On the second morning, the sun came up clear and about forty wagons pulled out with Charlie and me in the lead.

Taking out along the divide we crossed Council Creek and camped for the night about halfway between there and Stillwater Creek.

The next morning when we got to the creek we found that a bunch of enterprising cusses had made a bridge across it and were charging a dollar and a half a team for the use of the bridge. They had dug a hole in the old ford crossing and made it impassable.

Charlie and I were ahead of the other wagons so we were the first to find it out.

We told the men at the bridge that we would not pay that much and that some of the settlers did not have it to pay.

We camped and started fixing the old crossing.

The fellows at the bridge came over and warned us to stop or there would be trouble. They said, "We own the land and you will either have to pay or hook up and pull out!"

We just kept on working and told them to start all the trouble they thought they could handle.

By early afternoon the crossing was ready and the wagons were all on the other side of the creek and on their way again.

Charlie and I got home that night and put our horses into the barn before dark.

Three of the other teams stayed all night with us and pulled out in the morning.

A few days later another mover stayed all night with us and told us that the men at the bridge had destroyed the ford again and were doing a big business with their toll bridge. He said they were planning on coming down and giving us some trouble for helping the wagons across the ford.

It was a long ride for those boys at the bridge to come to see us, so Charlie and I oiled up our guns, filled our belts with ammunition, saddled up our ponies and went back to Stillwater Creek to see them.

But when we got there, they were as friendly as could be, and branded our informant as a liar.

They asked us to stay all night and have a little game of draw poker after supper.

Well, we had the little game and when Charlie and I left the next morning we were about three hundred dollars better off, but the men were good sports and took it without a squawk.

The toll bridge was there for a year before the settlers got together and built a bridge on the section line where the present bridge now stands.

It is now called the West Bridge and is on Stillwater Creek south of Stillwater, Oklahoma.

20 THE END OF AN ERA

ORPHA

A CIVIL WAR veteran named J. A. Miller had taken a claim about four miles east of Guthrie, Oklahoma.

He had four grown children — a son and three daughters — and I had known them for a long time.

The girls were all handsome, as fine as you ever saw.

The two older girls had married and left home but the youngest girl, Orpha, lived at home and helped her stepmother with the housework and her father with the farm work.

Orpha was one of the best and most beautiful women that God ever put on this earth. She was small, with a good figure, clear dark skin; rosy cheeks, perfect teeth and regular features. Her violet-blue eyes sparkled and danced and looked straight at you. Her wavy black hair laid in ringlets around her face and she had a loving, happy disposition.

On August 21, 1893, just before her sixteenth birthday, Orpha and I were married. It was a bright summer day and we were married under a big oak tree down on her father's farm.

Charlie Nida and I had finished our house the fall be fore and that spring we put in the crops. So I took Orpha to the little home down on the Cimarron.

Charlie stayed on with us for a while then he went to Colorado to ride for a cattle company.

Times were very hard; there was no work and no money.

293

Most of the time Orpha and I had only the bare necessities of life.

But we worked together, we had two beautiful baby girls and for seven years I knew what heaven must be like.

Then Orpha, who had always been so full of life, began to fail.

The doctor didn't seem to know what was the trouble at first, and we took her to other doctors.

She had the best medical help in the country and I watched over her day and night.

The doctors finally decided there was an abscess on her lung.

For three months she struggled and fought for her life.

As she grew worse I never left her.

I had been sitting in a rocking chair beside her bed for four days and nights. Holding her poor little thin hand and smoothing her hair from her forehead, I watched my world slipping slowly away.

Suddenly, a while after midnight of the fourth night, she said she wanted to sit up.

So I sat on the bed beside her and took her in my arms.

She put her arms around my neck and kissed me.

Then, looking up, she smiled and said, "Oh, is it day already? What a beautiful sunrise! Oh, what a beautiful light!"

She was gone.

There was no light.

I went out by the well and lay on the grass and cried.

I was alone with my two baby girls: Ethel who was four, and Faye, who was only two years old.

We buried Orpha in the cemetery here at Perkins, and there was a string of wagons and buggies over a mile long.

All the friends and neighbors were there with words of sympathy and offers of help.

Kind friends wanted to take my babies but I could not give them up; I could not bear to be away from them.

But after a few months I realized the babies needed a woman's care so I took them and went to my old friend and buddy, Rolla Goodnight.

Rolla had a ranch near Guthrie and he and his wife took us in and gave us a home.

Rolla's wife was a lovely woman and as good as she was handsome. She had a fair complexion, blue eyes and yellow hair that hung clear to her knees when she let it down to comb it.

She and Orpha had been good friends, and she loved and cared for my baby girls.

I helped Rolla with the ranch. Times were still hard but I got some work and we got along somehow.

The next year after I helped Rolla with the threshing and the harvest, I took the little girls and went down to my brother-in-law, Jim Morrow.

Jim's wife took care of them while I helped him put up his hay, husk the corn and pick cotton.

ANOTHER YEAR

My home place, down on the Cimarron, was rented out to a Texas man named Clate Johnson. His wife's name was Rosie and Rosie Johnson was a true Texas lady. She was always doing something nice for my baby girls.

They were very kind and wanted to help me all they could, so in the spring I went back home and lived with them and Rosie helped me care for the babies.

I broke out some new land on the place and grubbed out stumps and Clate farmed the old land in corn and cotton He was a good farmer and raised a good crop.

Times were still very hard and Clate and I cut wood and sold it in our spare time.

In the fall I went with Bill McKinley's hay baler.

ANNA

While I was working with Bill McKinley we went to bale some hay for L. O. Shannon. There was a girl working at his house named Anna Sillix.

I saw her the first night when I went in to supper.

She was a pretty girl with dark brown wavy hair and dancing brown eyes. She had on a dark skirt, a white shirtwaist and a big gingham apron.

When supper was over and the dishes were all done she sat down at the organ and played for us. She was a fine musician and I loved music.

We were there three days baling hay and Anna and I got acquainted.

Then one Sunday I took her for a buggy ride.

After that we went to the dances together.

296

Anna played for the dances and they came for miles to get her.

She would sit all night and play while I danced with the other girls but she very seldom danced.

After the dance we would get into the buggy and I would take her home; then I would drive on out to my place and take care of my team, cook breakfast and go to work.

Anna and I were married right here in Perkins and I took her out to my home on the Cimarron.

Anna loved and cared for my two little girls and was a wonderful mother to them.

She still played for the dances after our marriage and was the organist at the church for a long time.

One night George Gipson, an old Arkansas fiddler, came to our house and he and Anna played until midnight.

We were sitting by the fireplace having a sandwich before going to bed when I said, "I sure wish I could play a fiddle like you do, George!"

Anna said, "Send off and get you a fiddle, and I will teach you the notes and you can learn to be a good fiddler."

"No," said George, "send off and get the trimmings and I will make you a good fiddle."

So I sent away for the trimmings and George made the fiddle and Anna taught me to read music.

Anna used to play the organ and I played the fiddle and sang, but I never could get her to sing with me.

My two little girls grew up, and Anna and I had eight wonderful children of our own.

Life was not easy, but we always had each other and we were happy. The children were strong and healthy and they had plenty of room to grow.

We stayed there on the Cimarron for twenty-five years and fought cotton bolls and crabgrass.

Then we sold the farm and moved to Perkins, and I started a blacksmith shop.

THE END OF AN ERA

My old friend and father by adoption, Jasper Exendine, was down in Mexico for several years.

In 1907 he came back to Perkins and made his home with us.

His children came to visit him often and sometimes he went to see them. Jasper was a good man and he raised a wonderful family.

As he grew older he was very religious and he lived his religion every day.

Jasper was almost ninety-eight years old and had been with us for about three years when he went to visit a son who lived a few miles away.

He had been there only a few days when he died. When he left this old world he just lay down to sleep one night and that's the way they found him in the morning, with his hands crossed over his breast.

Jasper's funeral was both the white man's service and the old Indian rites.

Ben Hill, a full-blooded Delaware, preached the Indian sermon.

The Delaware language is not a written language but one of sounds. I had not heard it for years but before Ben Hill had spoken a dozen words I understood and could have repeated it as well as if it were in English.

Ben Hill began the service: "Wah ne Sha, Kee shel e min go [We thank Thee, God, for the privilege]. T al e mo hoot u qua [Now we come]."

When Ben had finished the white man gave his service.

When the white man's service was concluded at the grave, Ben Hill went up to the casket and with his pocketknife cut a hole in the top of the coffin underneath the lid.

Just a little bit of a notch, so the Great Spirit, Kee shel e min go, could get in after Jasper's soul.

Then he stepped back and the coffin was lowered. Ben raised his hand and said, "Jesus, Me laeg etch [Jesus, Amen]."

We all stood until the grave was filled.

An Indian never leaves a grave until it is full.

As we turned away the crowd divided into two groups, the friends in one group and the relatives in the other.

As Jasper's adopted son, of course I was with the relatives.

It is an old Indian custom that after the burial a meal is served to those who have come to the service, a meal consisting of bread and meat —in the old days, bread and venison.

So we ate our dinner there near Jasper's grave; his relatives in one group and his friends in another.

This is the Indian rite, part of the Indian religion.

As I sat on the ground sharing in this ceremony, I looked out over the waving grass and thought about the changes that had come since I first remembered Jasper.

It seemed that I was witnessing not only the end of the long and eventful life of my friend, but also the end of an era.

An era of adventure; often of hardship and danger. . . The era of the buffalo and wild deer, tall grass and longhorn cattle, Indians and Indian customs.

But the times were changing and that solemn Indian ceremony belonged to another day. The old Indian ritual was the symbol of another age.

De Cuta Mink Sha, Kee shel e min go [And now, God bless you].

# # #

Well, so long, partner. May the drought never hit your range. And may you always have a free horse and an easy saddle on the trail; with plenty of good grass and wood and pure sweet water at the Sundown Camp Grounds, is the wish of,

your old Cowhand

Frank Eaton
"Pistol Pete"

James A. Huebner
818 S.E. 4th. Street Suite 204
Ft. Lauderdale Florida 33301
Phone: 941/376-1595
Email: jahuebner@comcast.net

www.OldWestLawmansForgottenMemoir.com

Made in the USA
Middletown, DE
23 November 2017